Teaching Cats to Jump Hoops

OTHER BOOKS IN THE CULTURAL MEDALLION SERIES

Flowers at Dawn by Singai Ma Elangkannan
Penghulu by Suratman Markasan
Under the Bed, Confusion by Wong Meng Voon
The Earnest Mask by Xi Ni Er

Stories

YOU JIN

TEACHING CATS TO JUMP HOOPS

Translated from the Chinese by Sylvia Li-chun Lin

EPIGRAM BOOKS / SINGAPORE

 Published in Singapore by Epigram Books.
www.epigrambooks.sg

Originally published in 2004 by Lingzi Media as *Ting, Qing Chun Zai Ku Qi*

Cover illustration © 2012 by Esther Lim
Cover design by Stefany

Consulting Editor: Chua Chee Lay
Series Editor: Ruth Wan
Editor: Woo Wei-Ling

Published with the support of

NATIONAL ARTS COUNCIL
SINGAPORE

National Library Board Singapore
Cataloguing-in-Publication Data

You, Jin, 1950-
Teaching cats to jump hoops / You Jin ;
translated from the Chinese by Sylvia Li-chun Lin.
– Singapore : Epigram Books, 2012.
p. cm. – (Cultural medallion)

ISBN : 978-981-07-3657-6 (pbk.)
ISBN : 978-981-07-3658-3 (epub)

I. Lin, Sylvia Li-chun. II. Title. III. Series: Cultural medallion.
PL2908.N35893
895.13 -- dc23 OCN810344882

First Edition

10 9 8 7 6 5 4 3 2 1

For teachers, parents and students

Contents

PART ONE

Family Can Hurt You Too

The Shadow in Shackles 3

The Witch and the Fairy 15

Calling Out Repeatedly to the Good Boy 28

Cat and Pottery 47

PART TWO

Sensitive, Fragile Hearts

An Orchid in Bloom 61

The Wounded Grotto 74

Bruising from Love and Hate 89

Love Fool 100

The Boy with Golden Hair 109

PART THREE

Stumbling Stones on the Path of Study

Eggs Would Smile If They Had Feelings 125

Pets 137

A Fire Rages on the Exam Paper 146

Acknowledgments 155

PART ONE

Family Can Hurt You Too

The Shadow in Shackles

1

WHEN MRS. SEETOH walked into the staff room, her long face was a clear sign that a brewing storm was about to fill the building with wind. Sitting down heavily in the chair in front of my desk, she took out the notice I had distributed to the students the day before in relation to an upcoming camping trip and thrust it at me.

"My Zhuang Jing can't participate in this activity," she blurted out anxiously.

The three-day camping trip was an annual outing that the school had organised for its secondary three students. It was meant to bolster the students' interest in outdoor activities and give them a chance to exercise while fostering team spirit. Parents were generally supportive of the event, all except for Mrs. Seetoh, whose unhappy expression would have one thinking that we were forcing her daughter into doing something illegal.

"Zhuang Jing is a girl," she continued to sputter. "I can't allow her to spend a night away from home. Besides, with all those boys and girls mingling like that, who will take responsibility if something happens?"

"If something happens? What could happen?" I asked calmly.

Glaring fiercely at me, she retorted as if scolding a child, "With boys and girls sharing a room, how can you say they won't mess around?"

Mess around? How could she say something so distasteful?

"Mrs. Seetoh," I said sternly, "this activity has been organised by the school and the teachers will take full responsibility for student safety. Besides, boys and girls do not sleep in the same room, so there's no need for you to worry."

"That's enough!" she interrupted, and announced with a note of finality, "I will not allow my daughter to spend a night away from home."

That was my first encounter with Mrs. Seetoh. It was very unpleasant, to say the least. Our second meeting, however, was even worse.

2

Seetoh Zhuang Jing was a girl who left an indelible impression at first meeting. Although not an exceptional beauty, she had qualities uncharacteristic of girls her age: poise and quiet. Straight, lustrous, black hair, glossy as if glazed, framed an oval face that was unusually fair and clean. Her complexion was completely flawless. When she smiled, a tiny dimple danced subtly at the corner of her mouth, and light sparkled tantalisingly in her almond-shaped eyes which turned into crescent moons. This was why someone once teased that when Seetoh Zhuang Jing smiled, she toppled the whole class; and when she smiled again, the whole school crumpled. But she was stingy with her smile, and equally miserly with her words.

A loner who spoke little, Zhuang Jing was like an alien in the eyes of her classmates. Her baggy uniform blouse and calf-length skirt made her a campus laughingstock. Whenever the students had to form groups for team activities in class, she was always the odd girl out, which made for an awkward situation. More than once, I had asked the class monitor, Seow Chang Qing, to get the class to show some team spirit and include her in one of their groups, thinking that this might change her behaviour too. But each time, he simply scratched his head and rubbed his chin.

"She never says anything," he once replied helplessly. "She's like a block of wood, making it hard on everyone. And, and—" He laughed, looking hapless.

"And what?" I asked.

He scratched his head as he continued, "Sometimes we need to get together on a Sunday to discuss or gather materials for a project. Whenever we've rung her at home, her mother has treated us like criminals, interrogating us over and over as if she would only be satisfied if we told her our family history over eighteen generations. But that's not the worst part. What's terrible is, even after all the questions, she won't let Zhuang Jing out of the house. So to avoid trouble with her mother, no one wants Zhuang Jing in their group."

I sighed to myself. A problem mother was tougher to deal with than a problem student.

An only child and a loner on campus, Zhuang Jing was used to being alone, and was not at all bothered by the passive discrimination from others in the class. She drifted silently like a ghost on campus, with her shadow as her only company. She was an excellent student who consistently out-performed her class in school exams, although this was probably because she was so focused in class, with no leisure activities to distract her. Whenever her name was mentioned, her teachers would praise her unequivocally, all except me. I had a feeling that this girl, who had a youthful body but displayed no visible sign of youthfulness, lived like a shadow in shackles.

Once, I mentioned my impressions to a colleague, Li Hong, who shook her head like a rattle drum. "As the philosopher Zhuangzi once said, you're not a fish, so how do you know if a fish is happy?" she asked. "Even a shadow has its sorrows and joys. You think she's sad being a loner, but in my opinion, she enjoys being alone."

"It's probably not a choice she made willingly," I countered.

"If she really wanted a friend at school, her mother would be too far away to stop her," said Li Hong with a smile.

Nothing Li Hong said put my mind at ease. But I had no idea how to help the girl. As she was a good student with no disciplinary issues, her problems gradually receded to the back of my mind. That is, until after the midterm exams.

Surprisingly, Zhuang Jing's exam results in every subject were poorer than before. Her history teacher, Koo De Chen, told me that she had begun to show troubling signs a month before the exams. In the past her homework had always been neat and on time, but in the weeks leading up to the exams, she was late handing in her homework, which was sloppily done and clearly the result of perfunctory efforts. When Mr. Koo asked for a reason for her poor performance, she simply said that she was focusing on her weaker subjects, an explanation he'd accepted at the time. When all the students' results were in, however, he realised that she had done poorly not only in history, but in every other subject as well. Something was clearly amiss.

As her form and Chinese language teacher, I felt guilty for not noticing the change in Zhuang Jing—an obvious slip-up in my duty to the students. Before I even had a chance to talk to her, however, I was bowled over by a shocking event which soon occurred.

The period after the exams was always a tough time for teachers. We all wished that we could grow an extra pair of eyes or hands and that the hours in the day would double so that we could finish the mountains of work piled upon us. Just when we were all buried in paper and fighting for each extra second to finish our work, Chang Qing, the class monitor, ran breathlessly into the office and exclaimed anxiously, "Madam Tham, someone has taken my handphone from my bag!"

The students had all left for their physical education class, leaving the classroom empty and giving the thief the perfect opportunity. I immediately went to the classroom with Mr. Teo Yao Jin, our discipline master. All forty students were sitting like statues, their faces taut as drawn bows.

"Search their bags," Mr. Teo commanded sternly.

We searched the first row and found nothing. The second row also revealed nothing. When we got to the third row, I spotted a suspicious-looking face, a deathly pale face where the redness of the lips was swallowed by fear. It looked like a sheet of waterlogged paper, devoid of glow or lustre. Oh, it was Seetoh Zhuang Jing! My heart sank like a boat that had taken on water. Could this girl, who lived in a bungalow with her rich parents who drove a BMW, be a thief? As Mr. Teo and I stood next to her, her slender body shook uncontrollably, like a butterfly struggling to keep flight in a gale. Meanwhile, her hands clutched her expensive-looking cotton book bag so tightly that her knuckles turned white. The other students soon noticed her unusual behaviour, and the atmosphere quickly turned icy. She looked up at me, but it seemed as if she was staring down the barrel of a gun pointed at her heart. With a frightened and unfocused look in her eyes, she opened her mouth to say something, but whatever she wanted to say seemed stuck to her teeth and no sound came out. Although we had yet to search her bag, Mr. Teo and I were almost certain she was the culprit.

I softened my voice as I said, "Move your hands, Zhuang Jing. We need to search everyone's bag."

Instead of releasing her grip, she hugged the bag to her chest as if protecting a family heirloom. Tears streamed forlornly down her cheeks.

Mr. Teo signalled to me with his eyes. "Take her to the office," he whispered. "I'll join you when I finish here."

I took Zhuang Jing to the small room set aside in our staff room for consultations and sat her down on the sofa. Then I made her a cup of hot tea before sitting down myself.

"Zhuang Jing, the bag search is routine. There's nothing to worry about."

In a pained voice laden with anxiety, she spoke up suddenly, "Madam Tham, I didn't steal anything, I swear. If I did, I ought to be run over by a car the minute I walk out of school."

"Then will you let me look at your bag? You can return to class if I don't find something that shouldn't be there."

She clutched her bag even more tightly when she heard that, which upset me so much that I said, "If you keep this up, I think we'll have to call the police and have them search your bag!"

The same terror-stricken expression, as if a gun were being pointed at her heart, appeared on her face again, but this time she let go and placed her bag on the desk.

"Please, Madam Tham, I beg you. Please don't tell my mother."

I sighed silently as I opened her bag. Inside were neatly arranged textbooks and notebooks for each subject, but no handphone. I turned the bag inside out—still nothing. Then I noticed a secret compartment that had escaped my attention. Unzipping it, I slipped my hand inside and touched something that felt like a book. I took it out and one look gave me such a shock that I nearly jumped. It was a magazine of pornographic photos, with a cover showing a man and woman having sex, and page after page of them in various lewd sexual positions. I sucked in cold air and looked over at the girl. She was biting her bloodless lower lip, looking like a criminal awaiting a death sentence.

"Where did you get this?"

She was silent.

"Tell me, Zhuang Jing!"

It was a moment before she could manage an answer.

"From a friend."

"Which friend?"

She went quiet again, and remained that way no matter what I said.

3

Sitting in the principal's office, Mrs. Seetoh was the personification of a cold, glinting dagger. "It's a total fabrication to say that this filthy thing came from my Zhuang Jing," she said with a sneer. "When she came home, she told me that someone in her class had put it in her bag to get her into trouble."

"Zhuang Jing!" I looked at the girl with mounting anger. "Yesterday you told me it came from a friend of yours."

She didn't say a word, clamping her lips tightly and giving rise to an innocent-looking dimple. Mrs. Seetoh glared at me with her sleet-like eyes.

"My daughter would never have such disgusting friends! Use your head. I drive her to and from school every day. And once she's home, I seldom allow her out again, so where would she have gotten a chance to meet these so-called friends?"

But I had found the book in her bag. I should have taped her confession the day before, but it was too late for regrets now. An incident with ironclad evidence was now an unsolved mystery. Most disconcerting was the possible secret that lay behind it all: if Zhuang Jing was indeed a nice girl who was never let out of her mother's sight, then who could have given her the porn magazine? And why had her performance in school suffered so much that semester?

To get to the bottom of the matter, the school decided not to punish Zhuang Jing, and mother and daughter were led to believe that their explanation had been accepted. In the meantime, however, every effort was taken to find the answer.

First, I conducted meetings with individual students in the class. Several of them shared their impression that Zhuang Jing had been acting differently over the past month or two. In class, she was often absent-minded and sometimes even smiled into space. Several times when the teacher called on her, she had been so startled that she shot out of her chair. Woo Zhen Zhen, who sat next to Zhuang Jing, revealed that often when others were diligently taking notes in class, Zhuang Jing would be writing someone's name over and over in her notebook. She would write the same name repeatedly, all over her notebook until it was filled.

There was no doubt in my mind that she had fallen in love, but with whom?

While we were at the height of our investigation, something more startling than an 8.0 magnitude earthquake occurred.

One day during recess, I arrived at the staff room from my class to see Zhuang Jing waiting for me by the door, a dazed look on her face. One look made me cry out, "What's wrong?"

Her ashen face was overcome with utter dejection and her eyes had swelled up like plump peaches. "Can I talk to you alone, Madam Tham?" she asked.

We had just sat down in the side room when she began to wail. She cried herself hoarse, as if she were trying to cry her heart out, and blood seemed to drip from her voice. I kept quiet and let her weep. She cried for a very long time before I finally handed her a moist hand towel. After wiping her face, she looked up at me and said in a determined voice, "I want to die." Then she began to sob again. "Madam Tham, I don't want to live any more. I want to die."

I was shocked but reassured. Although she said she wanted to end her life, I knew that she wanted to live more than anything else. Someone who was ready to die was more likely to look for a tall building than to seek out her teacher.

I waited for her to calm down before saying, "Tell me what's going on. I'll do what I can to help you."

She went on to relate a story that was so unexpected, it seemed as if it had come straight out of *Arabian Nights*.

After years of being strictly controlled by her mother, Zhuang Jing felt like the walking dead. On the surface, she did everything her mother wanted and gave others the impression of poise, ease and contentment. Deep down, however, her resentment grew each day and her anger towards her mother surged like a stormy sea. Since her mother would not allow her to make friends at school, Zhuang Jing sought out other ways to meet people. A few months earlier, she had met an American boy in an Internet chat room. After a month of exchanging messages and photos, they had fallen madly in love. The young man then flew to Singapore to meet Zhuang Jing, and they agreed on an unusual way to see each other. At one o'clock each morning, she would unlock the door to her house and leave it ajar so that he could slip in. After enjoying a romp on the living room sofa, she would open the door to let him sneak out again. They spent two whole weeks this way without anyone finding out. The magazine found in her bag had been a parting gift from her boyfriend, Mike, before he returned to the United States.

Now the girl who had tasted the forbidden fruit discovered that a new life was growing inside her. Feeling helpless and alone, she came to tell me everything.

It was so sad and pitiful that a girl who had been shackled by her mother would rebel in such a way. With no one to guide her, she had fallen prey to an Internet con who called himself Mike. After swimming naked in the pool of desire for two weeks, he had disappeared in a puff of smoke. Only sixteen, she felt that she couldn't possibly spend the rest of her life dragged down by a fatherless child, and so abortion seemed like the only way out.

"Could you take me to have the procedure done, Madam Tham?" she asked in a quivering voice. "My mother will surely beat me to death if she were to find out."

The law in Singapore stipulated that parental consent was not required for abortions performed on girls who were above the age of thirteen. In recent years, defenders of traditional values had demanded amendments to the law, but the government had remained steadfast in its position, mainly out of concern that there would be a heightened rate of suicide and illegal abortions if the law were changed.

I wasn't sure what to say, and she began to cry again.

"If you don't help me, Madam Tham, I'll have to kill myself."

Thinking fast, I knew I had to agree to her request first and find a solution later.

I took her to the sick bay, where I asked a colleague on duty to watch over her. I told Zhuang Jing I was going to make arrangements at the hospital, but in reality I raced to report the matter to the school administration. An emergency meeting was convened and a consensus was reached: her mother had to be notified before we could even contemplate our next step.

I called Mrs. Seetoh and asked her to wait for us at her house.

"Has anything happened to my daughter?" she asked with palpable anxiety.

"We'll talk about it when we get there."

I put down the phone, jumped into the car, and rushed to their house with Mr. Teo.

"What's happened?" Mrs. Seetoh demanded the moment she saw us. "Why are people at school always picking on my daughter?" Then she became nervous when she noticed that her daughter was not with us. "What's happened to Zhuang Jing? Why isn't she with you?"

We told her everything. Her initial reaction was one of disbelief. She even loudly accused us of slandering her daughter, and threatened to sue us. When she finally believed us, however, she turned wooden from the shock.

"Mrs. Seetoh, you'd be driving her straight to her grave if you said anything critical right now. She's your only daughter, and you must do everything you can to help her get past this major obstacle in her life."

4

Mrs. Seetoh personally made the arrangements for her daughter's abortion.

I believed that it would be in Zhuang Jing's best interests to leave her rumour-rife environment and move to a different school where she could make new friends, continue her studies and have a fresh start. Zhuang Jing and her mother agreed with me, and with the school's recommendation, she made a smooth transfer to another secondary school.

The day before she left, I took Zhuang Jing to a fast food restaurant near our school for lunch. I ordered barbecued chicken for her. She had a good appetite and polished off three large pieces of chicken in no time. Sunlight streaming in through the windows landed on her fair, flawless face. As Zhuang Jing smiled shyly at me, her dimple danced quietly. She seemed to be brimming with dreams for the future. She had gone through a terrible ordeal, but with the help of people around her, she had been given a second chance. Of course there would be a scar, but it would fade with time and might even disappear one day. Most importantly, Mrs. Seetoh had learned a lesson she would never forget as long as she lived, and had changed the way she treated her child.

Shortly after Zhuang Jing's transfer, I read an exciting report in the newspaper: The Singaporean government was adopting multimedia sex education materials for lower secondary school students, who could begin to learn the correct approach to sexual relationships through innovative pedagogy. I approved this preventive approach.

A card from Zhuang Jing arrived around New Year's Day. In it, she had written, "Madam Tham, I really like my new school. I've made many friends, so please don't worry. I'll take good care of myself."

Sunlight remained quietly outside my window, but inside I could smell its sweet fragrance.

The Witch and the Fairy

1

THE EARLY MORNING sky was a vibrant blue, and the emerald green lawn was bathed in sunlight imbued with vitality. Like a sprouting mushroom, a dark shadow appeared suddenly on the scene. As I walked closer, I realised that the mushroom was shuddering.

It was a girl.

She was resting on her haunches. Her head was hanging so low that her long hair engulfed it, but I could see her shoulders heaving. She was sobbing and the profound, heavy sorrow seemed to weigh down the air around her.

It was the first week of school, a joyful time of welcoming new students. What had so upset this newly arrived junior college student to make her sob like that out there? To ask about the cause of her suffering at such a moment would have been to pour salt on her wound, so I crouched down and gently put my arm around her.

"Come, I'll take you to the sick bay," I said softly.

She shook her head, remaining as motionless as a fossil. But she could no longer hold back the flood of tears that spilled out as she collapsed on my shoulder. I stayed put and let her cry as much as she needed to. After a while, I said, "Come with me, let's go and freshen up." Perhaps exhausted from crying, she stood up listlessly, and I had to hide my shock when I saw her face. A large patch of her left cheek was blood red as if bruised, and the uneven surface resembled a lava field. It was a disconcerting sight. Without looking at me, she walked slowly with her head down, and when we reached the girls' restroom, she turned and bowed slightly. "Thank you," she said in a mosquito-like voice, "I'm fine now." I didn't believe her, but I had to respect her desire to be alone. So I let her go in by herself. Then I went to find a member of the Student Council and asked her to keep an eye on the sobbing girl.

Later, after speaking to a few students, I learned what had happened.

That morning, the junior college had hosted a big dance for the several hundred new students on the field. At first, boys had danced with boys and girls with girls, but soon the students began dancing with the opposite sex. After this girl made a twirl, she discovered, to her surprise, that her dance partner had fled in the rudest and most inconsiderate manner, leaving her frozen on the spot alone. The students who had witnessed the incident giggled, and a wicked boy even joked, "The prince was frightened off by the witch." After the dance, the new students filed into the auditorium for more orientation activities—everyone except her, who like a wounded animal, crouched in dejection, licking her wounds.

2

School started after a week of orientation activities. As luck would have it, the girl was placed in my class. She sat by the window. Long hair covered her left cheek, exposing the right side of her face which was pale and cold, like frost that had formed over thousands of years. Yet I knew that beneath that off-putting façade lay a heart which had never stopped bleeding, and it was my job to help the wound heal. But how was I to wrap the festering wound with the invisible gauze in my hands? Before finding the right strategy, I knew better than to make any rash moves, because a single misstep could make an irreparable mess of things.

I kept an eye on her. She was focused in class and meticulous with her homework, which she clearly wanted done with perfection. When I read her essays, I noticed that she preferred analytical topics. She had a logical mind and expertly wrote long essays that were well organised and convincingly argued—all evidence of her strong language ability and advanced analytical skills.

What bothered me was her reluctance to socialise. She kept quiet all day, like an ancient hermit who preferred isolation from the rest of the world. On those occasions when the class did group work, the other students would be in high spirits as they looked for partners. She, on the other hand, would sit impassively in a corner and ignore me no matter how hard I tried to talk her into joining a group. Every once in a while, she would force herself to sit with a group, but she would never participate in the discussion. While the other students would be engaged in animated conversation, she would act so aloof, she might as well not have been a member of the group. Sometimes she would even turn and look out the window at the sky or the clouds as if her group mates were transparent. This naturally upset the others, and they grew to dislike her. When they heard her name, they inevitably developed feelings of rejection. In the end, a vicious cycle was formed.

A week into the semester, the teacher in charge of co-curricular activities came to tell me that this girl, whose name was To Man-Ru, had not handed in an activity form. The rules of the junior college required every student to participate in at least one activity, but Man-Ru had ignored the teacher and refused to hand in her form. Since the teacher-in-charge didn't know what else to do, she came to see me.

I decided to begin by learning about Man-Ru's family background. After class that day, without informing Man-Ru, I called her mother and asked her to come and see me.

I was stunned when I saw Man-Ru's mother. She was a beautiful, middle-aged woman with delicate, flawless features that looked as if they had been painted. Her most attractive feature was her skin, which was smooth, glossy, clean and soft, like silk or jade or flawless marble. Mrs. To had no sooner taken her seat when she asked stiffly, "Has Man-Ru caused trouble again?"

"No," I said. "She's a good girl."

"Good girl?" She laughed softly and mirthlessly. "You're the first teacher to say that." She paused and frowned, then released a burst of talk. "I must have owed this child big time in my previous life. She has been tormenting me since the moment she was born. Why else would she have that big, ugly birthmark, which makes her look more like an unsightly ghost than a human? Do you know, her sisters are all pretty girls? But she's like an alien! With a face like that, it wouldn't be so bad if she were gentle and easy-going—but no, she's difficult. Everyone in our family suffers from her temper."

By then, it was clear to me that Man-Ru had a difficult time at home. Her family was quite obviously the breeding ground for her low self-esteem.

"Mrs. To," I said earnestly, "Man-Ru isn't very sociable. She seems quite unhappy. Do you think we could work together to help her gain some self confidence?"

"She has a worry-free life at home," said Mrs. To in a cool voice. "She eats what she wants and gets what she likes. What reason does she have to be unhappy? Her father spoils her simply because of her disfigurement. So what else does she want?" Her words had a hateful ring to them. "Nothing pleases her and she has no sense of gratitude. Day in and day out she's in a bad mood, and her teachers are forever complaining to me. What a headache."

As the saying goes, even a single word is excessive with people who don't share your view. This woman did not understand, and refused to enter, Man-Ru's inner world. It looked like our conversation had been a waste of time. But I received a glimmer of hope when she mentioned Man-Ru's father, so I called him the following day and asked him to come to school.

He was a big man with broad shoulders and a strong back. Two prominent dimples danced when he talked, which gave the impression that he was always smiling. When we met, he reached out and shook my hand vigorously.

"Man-Ru is a studious girl. She works hard at her studies, even though she does have a bit of a temper. Please don't be hard on her." He paused before continuing frankly, "Her fundamental problem is low self-esteem, which makes her unsociable. She and her mother don't get along very well, and I'm too busy with work to talk her around. Madam Tham, I truly hope you can help me."

With an understanding and open-minded father, I would not have to fight the battle alone any more, and I felt as if a heavy weight had been lifted off my shoulders.

I mentioned Man-Ru's refusal to take part in co-curricular activities. He considered the situation for a while, before saying, "She's a loner and not much of a talker. But she likes to read. Her English and Chinese are both quite good, so could you consider letting her join a reading group or something of that nature?"

What a terrific idea! I went ahead and urged her to join my Chinese language study group. To my happy surprise, she actually nodded and agreed without hesitation.

3

At the study group's first meeting, I wrote the title of their first essay, "My Self-Portrait", on the whiteboard and asked the students to try and convey a complete, unadorned picture of themselves on paper. Through this sort of self-analysis, I hoped to encourage them to understand both their positive and negative attributes.

Perhaps Man-Ru had been touched by my friendly attitude and genuine concern, because she was brutally honest in her depiction of herself in her essay. One section, in particular, seemed to have been written in tears:

"I am a scary witch. This is what my mother says and what others think of me. Heaven handed down a death sentence the moment I was born and I grew up under the repellent gaze of others. Love is an unfamiliar word to me. Sometimes I feel like killing myself, but I cannot bring myself to do it because I know it would hurt my father deeply. He is probably the only one who would shed tears over my death. I envy turtles and snails for their hard shells, which give them a place to hide when they are unhappy or need to escape the malicious gaze of others. They needn't worry even if the sky were to fall. I have no future. I study hard, but that is merely a way to pass the time as I have nothing else to do."

It was unbearably painful to read those words and I felt as if a needle had been thrust into my heart. Occupied with thoughts of the poor girl, I couldn't fall asleep that night.

After class the next day, I asked her to see me in the counselling office, where I'd laid out three eggs—a duck's egg, a salted egg and a century egg. When she sat down, I picked up a knife and told her to watch carefully. I raised the knife and sliced the first egg in half. After repeating the process twice more, I showed her the three different inner worlds of the eggs.

"Look," I said. She looked on with wide eyes.

"These eggs have no say in what they'll eventually become. Take the century egg, for example. It's inky black and has no beauty to speak of, but it doesn't give up on itself. Instead, it shuts itself in for self-cultivation until it creates its own unique beauty and glamour. Now everyone is taken by its delicious taste. Who would refuse to eat, or even taste, it because it's black and ugly?"

She didn't say anything, but a nearly imperceptible light began to slowly shine in her eyes. Inspiring words can sometimes exert tremendous, even life-changing, influence on intelligent people, and I knew I had to seize the opportunity and keep going. "Man-Ru, some things are predetermined in life, and we might not have the means, the ability or the power to change them. We need to face these things first, then accept them and finally forget their existence. Then we must try our best to discover and develop our good qualities. Sometimes self-confidence gives us a unique charm. Do you understand what I'm getting at?" She hung her head, not saying a word, but I could see that she was thinking and coming to some kind of understanding.

I have found that the rigid format of assigned essays can, over a long period of time, afflict more creative students with writing fatigue. So I decided to experiment with a series of more innovative and interesting curricula for the students in my Chinese language study group. I titled our first activity, which involved going out of the classroom and into the field for interviews, "Spring in Winter". I took the students to visit members of the Spastic Children's Association so the students could interview the children and write about their struggles. At the same time, I hoped to show how these disabled members of society were learning to support themselves and live independently, and disprove the misconception that they were worthless to society. To be honest, I'd also created the assignment with an unspoken ulterior motive: I was hoping that Man-Ru would open her eyes and see how she had magnified her own misfortune.

On the morning we arrived at the association, a gentle sun was weaving its thousands of golden filigrees into a net which sheltered the earth. The students walked spiritedly into the walled grounds as if they were going on a hike. The moment we passed through the gate, we were greeted by a patch of pleasing greenery on which some children with rigid muscles and uncoordinated movements were straining, and not always succeeding, to kick a ball with their stick-like legs. They were squealing with happiness. Quite a few children were standing around—some with hearing aids, some with thick glasses, some with a missing ear, and others who appeared mentally disabled. They were all staring blankly at us, the uninvited guests.

My students, who had been talking and laughing, were taken aback and grew silent when they entered this strange and unfamiliar world, coming face to face with this group of children who were less fortunate than themselves.

Before the visit, I had read everything I could find about the association and gave a detailed explanation to the students. There were many causes for the children's disabilities, but all were related to birth, particularly premature births. Premature babies' heads are too soft, which diminishes their breathing capacity, and this in turn affects their brain development and leads to convulsive disorders. Disabilities can also be caused by birthing complications such as a blow, a fall or prolonged labour. It can happen when a fetus is underdeveloped, or if the newborn infant contracts jaundice, high fever or meningitis. Over forty percent of the children at the association had underdeveloped brains. The Spastic Children's Association was formed to provide them with special education and skills training so they could learn to lead independent lives.

In one of the classrooms, we saw a teacher pointing to the letter *A* and tirelessly repeating it for a thin boy. His face was bathed in sweat as he forced his mouth and tongue to cooperate, but he kept failing to say it correctly. We were told that he had been trying to pronounce the letter for a month, but still had not managed to do so. In addition to impaired intelligence and poor eyesight, he also had twisted arms, which he could not use freely. He had a bad temper and often flew into a rage for no apparent reason. But his teacher had an endless store of patience in teaching, caring for and comforting the child. She hoped that he would know the world had not abandoned him simply because of his learning disabilities. Another child was having trouble controlling his hands. His teacher gave him a sheet of paper and a brush to dip in paint. Although it was placed right in front of him, his uncooperative hand kept moving to the left, and only after several tries did he manage to dip the brush into the paint can. His hand, however, refused to return to the paper, forcing him to smear the desk with dripping paint. Yet his teacher wore a smile the whole time, encouraging him and saying,

"It's all right. Let's try again."

These students had embarked on a long, hard road in their studies and might never reach their destination, but their teachers neither regretted their choice of profession nor complained about the exhausting work.

After special education, the children were sent to a small factory set up by the association to receive vocational training. We saw a teenage boy straining to carve a piece of wood, but his hand shook so violently that he kept missing his target and had to try over and over again. Yet he never lost his temper or gave up.

As she watched all this from the sidelines, Man-Ru suddenly lost control. In front of everyone, she began to wail, covering her face with her hands as tears streamed through her fingers. Gently putting my arm around her shoulder, I muttered softly, "Go ahead and cry, child. Cry as much as you want."

As we were leaving the association, Man-Ru, whose eyes were still red and puffy from crying, tugged at my sleeve and said, "Madam Tham, I'd like to volunteer here."

I nodded and said, "I'll make the arrangements for you."

4

From then on, Man-Ru volunteered at the Spastic Children's Association after school once a week, and I began to detect subtle changes on her face and in her mood. The differences weren't big, but I could sense that her low self-esteem was being replaced with confidence. The existence of the disabled children gave her a new understanding and view of her own misfortune, and she discovered her own self-worth by helping them. In turn, they grew more reliant upon her and for the first time in her life, she felt needed and valued by others. The friendly attitude of the staff at the association also gave her a chance to experience the joys and warmth of life in a community, which she found to be a new and sunlit world. Man-Ru continued to come and go on her own, but other teachers also noticed the change in her. As if she was an explorer who had discovered a new world, Miss Foo, who taught English, said to me one day, "Man-Ru used to live in a dark corner. She was like a porcupine whose hard, pointed quills made you uncomfortable, behaving as if the whole world was against her. But she's turned into a lovely girl this semester. I told a joke in class yesterday and she actually laughed! Sometimes, when we bump into each other, she even says hello first."

In the course of one's life, a person can be backed into a narrow, gloomy corner without knowing it. The corner can be so deep and dark that it seems like there's no way out, and a life can be wasted. But if an unexpected turn of events puts that person in contact with bright, sparkling sunlight, a change, with the strength to turn things around, is possible. That was what happened to Man-Ru.

The June school holidays were soon upon us. Before the holidays, I asked the students to share their vacation plans. They were understandably excited, vying for the chance to tell the class. Some would be working at fast food restaurants to earn some spending money; some would be travelling overseas with their parents; some had already made plans to have fun with their friends; and some intended to be bookworms and bury themselves in their studies. When it was Man-Ru's turn, she stood up confidently and said, "I've made a plan. I'll be helping out at the Spastic Children's Association. The association will be holding a large fundraiser at the end of the year, so there'll be lots to do." This piqued the interest of another student in the class, who asked, "Do they need more volunteers?"

Man-Ru turned to nod at the student. "The more the better," she said. A few other students, who thought the holiday was so long that they might get bored, also asked to participate. Man-Ru replied solemnly, "Maybe you should give it a try first."

When school was over that day, the students went with her to the association. I tagged along.

When the head of the association saw me, he gave me a thumbs-up sign. "I have to thank you for bringing us such an outstanding volunteer," he said with a smile as he took me aside. "Man-Ru not only works hard, she truly cares about these children. Love is really a panacea for them."

The students who tagged along that day were eager to help, and immediately signed up to be volunteers. Man-Ru showed them around like an older sister. The snail that had cowered inside its shell was now slowly sticking its antennae out.

School started again in July. What a pleasant surprise it was to see Man-Ru! She had cut her hair short, letting the world see her birthmark without trying to cover it up. She gave the impression that she was afraid of nothing, let alone the defect on her face. Man-Ru actually had nice features, but had looked unkempt in the past because she had covered half her face with her unruly hair, and her angry, gloomy demeanour had only made her appearance even more disagreeable. Now a confident glow shone on her face, turning her into a real charmer.

She was obviously in a good mood when she saw me.

"Are you free this Saturday night, Madam Tham?"

"Is something going on?"

"Yes, the association is hosting a celebration, and I was wondering if you could make it."

Of course I would go—even if it snowed or the ground frosted over.

The celebration was held in the association's auditorium, which was packed with people. Everyone laughed when the silvery screens were pulled apart. A dozen children dressed in bright clothes, looking like colourful flowers, lit up the stage with happiness. One of them, a tall girl, wore a colourful hat and multi-coloured clothing. Makeup exaggerated her facial features, giving her an especially large mouth with upturned lips that made her look happy, even though she wasn't smiling. When the music started, she led the other children in dancing to the music. All of them moved differently. They were never in step, but that could not hide the joy they felt deep down inside. In fact their joy, like an unstoppable flood, was contagious—parents in the audience were tearing up. I felt my heart beat faster as I watched, and I sat up straight in my seat. Squinting to get a better look, I saw that the girl who had completely lost herself in the dance was in fact Man-Ru.

Happy tears misted my eyes.

The girl who had once been called a witch was now happiness personified in the melodious music, transformed into a fairy descending from heaven.

Calling Out Repeatedly to the Good Boy

1

THE MORNING I saw the notorious Tay Heng Yong in my class, my initial reaction had been one of surprise. I looked again and still could not believe my eyes, for he had shed his hooligan airs, and he couldn't have appeared more different from his former nasty and violent self.

He was sitting at the first desk by the window. Sporting a crew cut, he had big, round, onyx-like eyes that gave off a pure, innocent sparkle. His thick lips curved upwards slightly as if he didn't have a care in the world, and the hint of a smile crept naturally out of the corners of his mouth.

Six months before, while attending another school, he had made headlines in the national newspapers in the wake of a gang fight. His school had hosted a basketball game which his team had lost. As captain, he was so incensed over the humiliating defeat that he had gathered a few of his friends and beat up members of the winning team after the game at a bus stop near the school gate. They weren't fooling around; they had meant to hurt. By the time the police heard about it and raced over, two of the winning team's players were already lying on the ground, bleeding from head injuries. The incident shook the school system, and appeared the next day in the local section of the newspaper under the headline: "Dispute over basketball game: Blood spilled at school entrance."

Heng Yong, barely sixteen at the time, was sentenced to two years in Singapore Boys' Home.

For the first six months, Heng Yong's good behaviour so impressed the Boys' Home director that he was allowed to continue attending regular classes at school in the morning and return to the Home after class in the afternoon. The director, however, urged him to transfer to another school so that he would not be the target of criticism, and more importantly, so that he would stay away from bad influences.

That was how and why Heng Yong transferred to my school and into my class.

He was enrolled in the Normal Stream of Secondary Four. The arrival of a resident of the Boys' Home immediately intimidated some of the other students who usually liked to stir up trouble. Feeling dwarfed by his presence, these students now behaved themselves and stopped goofing off. The good students, on the other hand, considered Heng Yong a criminal and warily steered clear of him. An uncomfortable chill was added to the already sombre classroom atmosphere.

Clearly I had been handed a ticking time bomb, which if handled correctly, could actually be turned into living teaching material, an excellent example to the other students. I hated to think of the consequences, however, if the bomb went off.

I decided that doing nothing was the best course of action, and pretended that nothing was amiss. Opening my textbook, I began class as if it were any other day. When the students saw my indifferent demeanour, they looked around quizzically. A talkative boy in the middle row could not hold back. "We have a new student, Madam Tham," he reminded me in a soft voice. I nodded slightly, a non-reaction that prompted him to look in the direction of the window and make a face. "A famous one too," he muttered. I ignored him and turned to the whiteboard to write down a few proverbs that the students had studied before, to check their comprehension. As the students answered my questions, I stole a glance at Heng Yong. He was busy, with his eye on the board, his ears pricked, his hand writing down the phrases and his mind committing them to memory.

Class was soon over. Before the bell rang, I used the last couple of minutes to introduce Heng Yong to the class. "Tay Heng Yong is a transfer student," I said. "I hope you will honour the spirit of helping each other and welcome him. I'd like everyone to help him adjust quickly to the new environment."

I walked out as the bell rang. Heng Yong got up from his seat and raced to catch up with me. The strong smell of cigarettes enveloped me suddenly like a rank whirlwind, making me dizzy. When he stood close to me, I noticed a short but deep scar under his left eyebrow. Resembling a tiny dagger, the scar reminded me of the Chinese saying "Clean knife in, bloody knife out" and its association with sinister stories of the underworld.

"Madam Tham, I'm sorry I can't attend the remedial session this afternoon or any other afternoon in the future," he said respectfully.

"I know, you have to return to the Home after class." I nodded in understanding. When he opened his mouth to speak, I noticed that his teeth were dirty and yellow, covered with unsightly cigarette stains. As he was turning to walk away, I asked with a smile, "Are you a heavy smoker, Heng Yong?"

He scratched his head and smiled shyly. After a while, he finally said, "I—um—over there—I mean, at the Boys' Home, the rules are very strict. I hadn't even smelled cigarette smoke for at least six months, so now that I'm out, I have a few to ease the craving."

"What brand?"

He gave me the name of an established cigarette brand.

"Oh, they're not bad. They have a minty taste," I said.

"Do you smoke, Madam Tham?" he asked, the light of pleasant surprise shining in his eyes.

I smiled. "I did when I was very young, but only for a while. To me, smoking is like eating durians. It smells wonderful when you're eating them, but a stink clings to you after you're done. The stink was too much for me, so I quit."

Rather than lecture him about school rules, I tried to share my feelings as someone who had been in a similar situation. This was something new and interesting to him, and it erased the distance between us. He laughed freely, looking like a young boy who had yet to experience the ups and downs of life. It was a tender, endearing sight to behold.

"Madam Tham, there's a new product that eliminates the cigarette smell," Heng Yong said. He took out an aerosol can, opened his mouth and sprayed something inside. Instantly a light, minty fragrance drifted from his mouth in a shapeless, green cloud. "I sneaked a cigarette into the bathroom and forgot to use this," he said in a low voice as if letting me in on a secret.

Smoking cigarettes is like the urge to gamble—easy to start and hard to stop. I wanted to help this boy quit, but I knew the road ahead would be long and the responsibility weighty.

The next day in class, I assigned an essay topic that would allow Heng Yong to speak his mind freely: "The Thing I Regret Most".

Everyone began to write, and the room was quiet except for the sound of pens scratching paper. I watched Heng Yong as he cupped his cheek in deep thought. After twenty minutes, he finally picked up his pen. Then he wrote non-stop, one page after another as if a levee had been broken by an unstoppable flood. When the bell rang, quite a few students still hadn't finished. They asked if they could turn in their essays at the end of the school day, and I readily agreed.

When school was over that day, the class monitor collected the essays and placed them on my desk. I could hardly wait to read Heng Yong's essay. I was surprised to see that several pages of his new exercise book had been torn out, and so carelessly that the edges were jagged. Puzzled, I flipped through his exercise book until a piece of paper fell out.

"I understand your intention behind the topic, Madam Tham. I wrote about the one thing that I regret most but it was merely a story, not a genuine reflection of how I feel inside. I didn't want to deceive you, so I tore the pages out. I don't think there's anything regrettable in my life, for what I've gone through has been predestined by fate."

Fate! He actually blamed all his mistakes on fate!

Realising that this was a delicate situation, my heart felt weightless and dislocated as if it had been plunged into an unfathomable abyss.

It has been my lifelong conviction that behind every problem student lies a problem family. So I called Heng Yong's mother and asked her to see me.

We had settled on two o'clock in the afternoon, but she was an hour late. Obviously rushing to get there, she was panting hard. The moment she arrived, she began to apologise profusely as she wiped the sweat off her face, looking anxious and apprehensive. I sized her up. She had a large, round and flat face that was oily and wet with perspiration. Trailing her was the nearly imperceptible smell of grease, like deep-fried salted dough cakes that had just been fished out of a pot. Her hair, which was greying here and there, was most unusual. From a distance, one got the impression that she was wearing a spider web on her head.

"You must've been busy," I said, showing her to a seat.

"Yes! Yes!" She nodded almost frenetically. "A whole slew of customers came in at once and I couldn't get away. That's why I'm an hour late. I'm really sorry."

I learned from our conversation that she and her husband ran a hawker stall at a coffee shop in Queenstown. Every morning, they got up before sunrise to steam, boil, stir-fry, slow-cook, bake and fry, preparing a few dozen dishes that were then placed on aluminium trays for customers to choose from.

"Sometimes we're so busy, we barely have time to breathe." She wiped her face as she continued, "Heng Yong is our only child, and I had him in my thirties, so now all I want is to make enough money for him to enjoy a good life. You don't know how his father spoils him. If he doesn't like what he's given at dinner, he flips his plate upside down, sending food all over the place. His father races into the kitchen to make him something else."

I was so stunned that my jaw dropped.

Taking no notice of my expression, she continued to chatter away, "Now that he's in the Boys' Home, he can no longer eat good food, so he's become all skin and bones. It pains me to see him like that. The boy's downfall is his honesty. After the fight, he shouldered all the responsibility at the police station. I told him he should've told the police that he'd only been an onlooker and hadn't been in the fight. It would've been fine if he'd denied everything, but he wouldn't listen to me. He even said something about a man taking responsibility for his actions. So you see, how could an honest boy like him not always get the short end of the stick?"

Words cannot describe how I felt as I listened to her.

The source of Heng Yong's problems was sitting right in front of me. No good fruit can grow from poor soil, and a plot of land overrun with insects will only be able to yield worm-infested produce.

Heng Yong was the typical product of blindly indulgent parents. But his problems were worse than other teenagers, because in addition to material comforts, his family gave him misguided ideas on how to get by in the world, and would let him get away with murder.

How in the world was I supposed to go about tending to and fertilising this insect-infested sapling?

I sank into deep thought, searching for an answer.

2

In class I assigned an engaging exercise. Using "cigarette smoking and life" as the central theme, I asked the students to come up with slogans and illustrations of their own design. They loved the idea, and began brainstorming for ideas and designs with great enthusiasm.

After collecting the students' exercises, I checked their work slowly. There were many innovative pieces. One student, for instance, had drawn a ferocious beast with a man whose lower body had been swallowed dangling between its cruel, crooked fangs. The victim's upper body was struggling. His arms hung outside the beast's mouth to personify helplessness, powerlessness, fear and panic; yet the man's right hand was still clutching a pack of cigarettes, and several of the cigarettes were depicted falling out of the crumpled package. The eerie, white cigarettes gave the drawing a heightened sense of creepiness. The drawing came with the caption "I must eat eight smokers a day" to highlight how smoking unavoidably leads to death. It was a creative image, rich with meaning. Similarly, the other students followed my instructions to convey the negative impact of cigarette smoking using images and captions; all except for Heng Yong, who had written a single line: "Great strength can uproot a mountain; imposing airs can subdue the world". Beneath his caption, he had drawn a brawny giant with one hand holding a mountain in its palm with great flair. Between the middle and index fingers of the other hand was a lit cigarette, with its smoke curling upward. The piece met the standard and demands of a professional advertisement. This Heng Yong was quite something. Apart from his talent in drawing, I was impressed by his precise and concise use of language. He clearly had literary potential.

After some time and plenty of thought, I located a terrifying and disgusting colour illustration in a medical journal. It depicted one hand holding a red blood vessel that was being squeezed by the other hand. Flowing from one end of the vessel were streams of yellow, green, brown and black substances, showing the toxic chemicals that had accumulated in the vessels of a chain smoker. I cut out the image, along with a photograph of a late-stage lung cancer patient, who was gaunt and skinny as a rail. It was a ghastly image of someone who barely looked human. The photo was accompanied by the patient's heartfelt thought: "I won't touch a cigarette in my next life." I glued the two images side by side and added the subtitle, "A year ago, great strength could uproot a mountain and imposing airs could subdue the world. A year later, the strength is gone and the mountain topples, covering the body in dirt".

Then I went to the supermarket to buy some candy with a heavy fruit fragrance that lingered in the mouth of anyone who ate them. I believed this would be a good aid to quitting smoking.

When everything was ready, I asked Heng Yong to come to the staff room, where I returned his homework along with my masterpiece. I watched his reaction. He looked at the two, scratched his head out of habit, and then began to laugh soundlessly. I handed him the bag of candy and said, "Heng Yong, why not give quitting a try? It'll be hard, but you must keep at it and not lose heart. Doesn't the name Heng Yong represent your personality and potential—*heng* for perseverance, *yong* for courage? What you have is perseverance and courage, and this courage lasts forever, do you understand?"

He looked at me pensively and nodded. "It's hard to break an old bad habit," he said. "Really hard. In addition to perseverance and courage, patience and time are also paramount. Before I went to the Boys' Home, I smoked three or four packs of cigarettes a day. Each time the discipline master caught me, he would cane me in front of everyone. He beat me till I was numb, but after a while it stopped being a big deal. Later I even had an ongoing bet with the other students: If I finished a whole pack before the discipline master caught me, they'd give me ten dollars; I'd give them ten if I was caught, plus a free show."

"What kind of free show?" I was puzzled.

"Public caning," he replied with a smile. "I nearly died from the lack of cigarettes during my first few weeks in the Boys' Home. But I didn't die, so I vowed to spoil myself and smoke to my heart's content once I was out."

If scolding and caning could not help him understand the problems with smoking, then any punishment would be a waste of time and effort.

I fixed my gaze on him. Drawing out every word, I said, "Heng Yong, you must gain a thorough understanding of the crippling effects of cigarettes' slow poisons before you try to convince yourself to eliminate the harmful craving once and for all. As the saying goes, heaven helps those who help themselves. Only you can help yourself."

He looked down at the candy I'd given him. A faint smile flitted across his face.

"I'll try, um, try to smoke less. Please give me time."

I nodded and changed the subject. "Are you doing all right at the Home?"

"I hate it." A look of extreme loathing appeared on his face. Not usually much of a talker, he now began to speak animatedly. "It's bad enough to lose your freedom, but in there you lose your dignity too. The overseers yell, scream and curse at us for the smallest infraction. They make us exercise almost to death. In there I feel no different from an animal, except that an animal probably eats better and lives more comfortably. It's an unfair world. Why should the worst of the worst be allowed to roam freely while I'm sentenced to two years for nothing more than picking a fight?" He grew so agitated as he spoke that he probably would have pounded the desk if not for the ringing of the school bell, which brought him back to the present. He continued in a soft, weak voice, "I accept my fate now, Madam Tham. I believe that one or more inescapable karmic obstacles exists in every person's life, and that being sent to the Boys' Home is one of mine."

The more I listened to him, the more disconcerted I felt. Apparently Heng Yong hadn't learned anything from his mistake, which he blamed on fate. For the time being, he followed the school's rules

—except for smoking—and his homework was always neat and on time. One day, when I praised his behaviour in front of other teachers in the staff room, my colleague, Mr. Teo, said with a sneer, "Heng Yong is simply acting. He's using his classes as an excuse to gain half a day of freedom. He's not really into studying." On reflection, I realised that Mr. Teo may have been right.

I asked Heng Yong, "Do you really believe that detention for you is a karmic obstacle and not a punishment?"

Seeing the stern look on my face, he held his tongue.

Devious people who harbour evil intentions cause trouble everywhere they go. They commit all sorts of evil deeds for personal gain, even when they know that their actions bring pain to others. But some develop an unhealthy attitude towards life at a young age because their indulgent parents instil in them a value system that looks good on the surface, but is in fact misguided. Hence this boy who had strayed seemed intent on heading down the wrong path, when he was actually being pushed in that direction without realising it. Worse yet, he was completely unaware of his situation—hurt by what was going on around him, he didn't realise that he was his own worst enemy. If I wanted to do something for him, my most urgent task would be to help him rediscover the right value system and the proper attitude towards life. But as the saying goes, it takes ten years to grow a tree, and a hundred years to form a person. It is difficult to straighten a twisted steel bar—very difficult indeed.

My immediate and most daunting obstacle was time. Every day after class, Heng Yong's father picked him up and drove him back to the Boy's Home. This meant that I had limited time at school to teach and get close to him. The prospect of having a positive influence on him was pitifully weak. Nevertheless, I usually conducted our conversations in a light-hearted manner, and I could tell that he appreciated my effort and concern, because he was fairly open with me. In a word, we developed a good student-teacher relationship. Sometimes when I passed him in the hall, I would ask with a smile, "How many yesterday?" He always knew what I was getting at. Once he raised five fingers. "Too many," I said, pretending to be upset. "Can't you try to smoke less?"

He smiled. "I'm working on it. Please give me time."

Confucius said that you should teach a person based on his ability. In fact, when dealing with a problem student, one also needs to guide him based on his personality. Heng Yong had been spoiled since childhood, so I would have met with resistance if I'd adopted sharp language and a heavy-handed approach to force him to change.

I later discovered that he liked to sit alone in a corner of the campus and lose himself in martial arts novels during recess. When I brought it up, he told me that life at the centre was so monotonous and boring that martial arts novels helped him to while away the free time before he had to go to bed, and subsequently he had become hooked on them.

Pleased to learn that he enjoyed reading, I began buying him books, pile upon pile of books, mostly biographies of famous people. I wanted to help him find his goal in life by reading about these people's hardships and struggles. Most of all, I wanted him to understand and appreciate my intentions, that he would at least become an upright person if not a great, accomplished man.

All my efforts and plans, however, were in vain. He turned out to be a terrible disappointment.

3

One morning, I walked into the classroom to find Heng Yong's seat empty.

That was unusual, since absence in class meant that he'd have to sit quietly all morning at the Boys' Home, which he detested. As Mr. Teo had said earlier, Heng Yong "loved to use studying as a pretence to gain half a day of freedom."

I called his house and his mother answered. She was incoherent, and it was clear that she was in tears. In fact, she was crying so much, I couldn't understand what she was saying, apart from something about a police station. Could he have gotten into trouble again? And could it be so serious as to involve the police? I told her I would stop by after class, and was surprised to see her show up at school an hour or so later. She was sitting in the reception room—her hair a mess, her eyes puffy, with an expression of utter dejection. When she saw me, tears began to fall again, until she was sobbing so violently that she nearly choked. It took some time and self-control before she finally managed to say, "It's my fault, Madam Tham, it's all my fault."

It pained me to see someone tear herself apart like that. I handed her some tissues and made coffee as I waited for her to calm down. Then I asked her what had happened.

It turned out that several nights before, when she and her husband had returned home after closing up their stall, they found to their horror that they had been burgled. The intruders had turned their place upside down and walked off with over ten thousand dollars in cash that Heng Yong's parents had yet to deposit in the bank. They called the police, who suspected there was more than met the eye, because there were no signs of forced entry on the doors or windows. After a thorough investigation, the police quickly arrested two unemployed youths and proved that, indeed, something else was going on—the mastermind was the victims' own son, Heng Yong.

Amid tears and sniffling, his mother said, "Everything would have been fine if I hadn't called the police. It's my fault. I deserve a thousand deaths. I've ruined my child's future! I delivered him straight to the police. I'm the stupidest woman on earth. I'll never forgive myself." She blew her nose and continued, "Please help me, Madam Tham. Help me plead with the police. Please tell them that Heng Yong is a good boy and a good student. Please ask them not to extend his sentence, please."

The heart she lay bare before me had been shattered by her unfeeling son. Yet despite her deep pain and open, bleeding wound, she was ready to fight the people who were charged with putting her child away in the name of justice. She would not allow anyone to harm a hair on her son. How stubborn, profound, helpless and foolish parental love can be!

I felt sorry and awkward when I asked, "Did you ask Heng Yong why he needed such a large sum of money?"

"He wanted to borrow eight thousand dollars from me earlier to help a friend get through some hard times. I didn't give it to him, because it was an awful lot of money and I was afraid we might not get it back. But who would've thought—" Her sorrow got the better of her and she began to wail again. "I didn't expect that he, that he'd give our house key to his friends. Madam Tham, if, if I'd known he would take such drastic actions, I'd have given him the money, and nothing would have happened. It's all my fault. I've ruined my own child."

As I listened to her, I felt profound pity and sorrow spreading through my heart, like ink drops bleeding onto rice paper. She had indeed ruined him, due to indiscriminate indulgence that deprived him of a sense of direction and sent him into a downward spiral. Heng Yong's seemingly honest, innocent face floated up from my memory.

I couldn't stop my own tears from welling up.

4

In the wake of the burglary, Heng Yong lost the freedom to attend school at all. Two months later, a judge re-sentenced him to two years in a juvenile reformative training centre. The only consolation was that he could still attend classes, and then sit for the national exams at the centre.

After he left, I felt an ache in my heart whenever I saw his empty seat. It hurt, but since there was no remedy for the pain, I just let it be.

Months after his departure, his mother showed up unannounced one day. Her hair was now completely grey as if she had come out of a snowstorm. Even her eyes seemed to glaze over as she stood awkwardly by my desk.

"I've been to campus a few times, but couldn't find you before," she said.

"Why didn't you call and make an appointment?" I pulled up a chair for her and said, "Here, have a seat."

But she refused to sit. Instead, with her head lowered, she said, "Heng Yong told me I must find you and tell you something on his behalf."

I was all ears.

"He wants me to apologise to you."

"Apologise?"

"Yes," she said meekly. "He wants to say he is sorry."

He was sorry. He wanted to tell me he was sorry.

So he had not blamed his present situation on fate. Finally, he'd realised that he'd done something that he needed to apologise for. From those three simple words "He is sorry" I was pleased to see a light in Heng Yong's future. However, I could not help feeling that he should have apologised to his mother and not to me. And his mother should have apologised to him. They had caused each other a great deal of pain and suffering.

In all fairness, Heng Yong wasn't a bad person in terms of his nature or personality, but his family environment had allowed him to commit errors time after time without any real consequences. Even after he'd made grave mistakes, his parents still tolerated and indulged him. Unable to tell right from wrong, he'd ended up living his life in murky water. Someone had to thump him to wake him up. Then, and only then, would he be able to understand how his mistakes had caused him such great pain. Now that he was in the reformative training centre, the place he feared most, it was time for him to face the wall and repent. On the other hand, if no one showed him any warmth and concern at a time when he could sink no lower and everyone considered him a bad person who deserved to be where he was, he might become cynical. In that case, once he was released, he could easily turn to a life of crime.

So I began buying books for him once again. I sent him all sorts of motivational books to encourage him and let him know that someone was thinking of him beyond the dark, dank walls of the centre. Most importantly, he had been on the brink of drowning, and I hoped that these books on self-improvement would be the driftwood that could help him swim to shore.

I wrote to him frequently, calling him a good boy each time. I believe that once a person gets used to a term of address, he naturally turns into a person who lives up to that term.

Good boy, good boy, good boy, good boy. Good boy, good boy, good boy, good boy.

I called out silently when I thought of him. I called it out repeatedly, never tiring of calling him a good boy.

5

After a long year of diligent studying, Heng Yong finally had a taste of the sweet instead of the bitter when he passed the national exams at the juvenile reformative training centre.

His mother made a special trip to tell me when the results were announced.

"He received excellent marks in several subjects, earning an overall score of eighteen!"

Her once greasy, fleshy face looked like a dance floor that had just been waxed, and it sparkled brightly. I found her happiness infectious.

Eighteen! With a score like that, he would be accepted into many good schools.

"When can he go home?" I asked.

"Soon, very soon." She was so pleased that she was nearly incoherent. "With good behaviour, he's eligible for early parole. He'll be out in maybe a month or two."

I barely recognised Heng Yong when he came to see me at school.

He looked lean and fit. His skin, however, was a pale white, probably from spending long hours indoors with little exposure to the sun. His fair skin made his onyx-like eyes appear especially bright and expressive. Gone was the lingering stink of cigarettes.

What surprised me most though, were his teeth. The yellow, nicotine-coated teeth now gleamed like clean, white china.

"How many yesterday, Heng Yong?"

He laughed when he heard that.

"Zero. You'll never have to ask me that question ever again. The answer will always be zero. I've quit smoking for good. Do you know that I went to a dentist and got a thorough cleaning the day I left the centre?" He paused. "Yesterday, one of my mother's friends came to see her. He was chain-smoking in front of me, and I felt no urge at all. My craving is gone and I'll never touch another cigarette again. I made mistakes in the past because I had a demon in my heart. But now I have a thorough and deep understanding of myself, and I refuse to be a slave to the demon. I want to be the master of my own fate."

I spread out a newspaper article I had been keeping with me.

"Read it," I said. "Go ahead, read it yourself."

The article was a special feature about how a rich man in Hong Kong had made his fortune. In 1982, a man named Chan Cheuk Yin had robbed a bank in Wanchai, for which he received a fifteen-year sentence. But he studied hard and became the first person in Hong Kong to complete his university education in prison. After he was released, he worked hard, started his own business, and was now Chairman of the Board of many corporations in Hong Kong. He could have anything he wanted—good wine, fancy cars, beautiful women, anything.

Heng Yong read the article carefully and looked up. "That's not the kind of life I want, Madam Tham," he said, pursing his thick lips.

His comment took me by surprise.

Pointing at the picture of the impressive-looking and well-dressed rich man, he gave me a detailed and logical analysis: "This Mr. Chan worked hard to start a business after he was released, but he was after material comfort. I believe that spiritual happiness cannot be bought with money. I've done many things that have hurt my parents, and I'm going to make it up to them even if it takes me the rest of my life. After I got out, some of my old friends came to see me and I went out with them. But to be honest, I didn't enjoy it. On the other hand, I'm happy and gratified when I help out at my parents' stall, where I can spend time with them and talk about trivial things. I've applied to study Information Technology in polytechnic. I hope to find a steady job after graduation so I can support my parents with the fruits of my own labour."

I felt I no longer had to worry about him after hearing such thoughtful comments.

Heng Yong had finally truly ridden himself of the demon in his heart. He was no longer like an ostrich burying its head in the sand to avoid temptation, or a fox dressed in a beautiful coat that lacks real substance. He was an armoured warrior—well-prepared for and unafraid of any hardship or temptation. He would stride confidently and bravely towards his life's goals.

"Thank you, Madam Tham." He reached out to shake my hand. His thick hand was callused, reminding me that his heart was probably covered in a callus thick enough to repel all sorts of venomous creatures.

With true sincerity, I replied, "Good boy, best of luck."

"Take care of yourself, Madam Tham. Don't work too hard."

Through moist eyes, I looked at his receding back, silently reciting, "Good boy, good boy, good boy…"

He soon reached the gate, where as if responding to my call, he spun around and waved with happiness and confidence.

Cat and Pottery

1

TODAY I DESIGNED a fun exercise for the class. On the surface it was an activity related to Chinese language, but my real purpose was to probe the students' inner worlds.

After handing out small slips of paper, I told the students to write a single phrase that best reflected their desires. Before they began, I reminded them to think deeply and carefully and to avoid rash, careless writing. Some scratched their heads, some tugged on their ears, and some chewed on their nails as they searched deep within themselves before putting pen to paper. They handed in their phrases when they were finished.

When I got home that night, I sat under a desk lamp and gave the slips of paper a good read. The faces of my students, which showed a range of emotions and personalities—happy, sad, quiet, impish, stern or carefree—floated up in my mind. Their desires were simple and direct. Those with low marks wished to be the top student in their class; those from poor families hoped for sudden wealth; homely ones wanted to be pretty; those with a weak foundation in languages yearned for mastery of both the Chinese and English languages and so on; except for one paper, on which only a three-syllable word was written: "Possible".

Possible? What did that mean? Try as I might, I could not understand its meaning. I checked the name—ah, Pang Yu Zhou.

Yu Zhou had caught my attention shortly after the semester began. He had a pointed face which was so fair that it looked like a freshly steamed bun, and his eyes were incongruously black as if glazed. Sitting quietly in class, he resembled a grave-looking snowman on a late winter field. When I spoke to him, he stared back with an expressionless face, but his darting eyes betrayed a highly unstable inner world. This sixteen-year-old boy had obviously donned a mask to cover up whatever was going on in his mind. I tried to talk to him, but he was miserly with his words, as if his every utterance was a rare treasure to bestow. Yu Zhou was always well-behaved, however, and although his performance in class was never outstanding, his homework was always neat and on time. His record was free of infractions such as skipping class or being absent without permission, getting into fights or causing trouble, which was why I made no further attempt to find out what was going on with him. Instead I let him live quietly and peacefully in his little world.

I did, however, tell him to see me after class the next day. When he arrived, I pulled out his slip of paper and asked with a smile, "What does this word mean?"

With his head bowed low, he pursed his lips and kept quiet. Instead of forcing him to talk, I sat and waited patiently. What seemed like a century passed before a sudden change erupted on his wooden face. In a defiant and unhappy tone, he said, "No matter what I do, my mother always says it's impossible for me to succeed."

This simple sentence exposed a wound that had been festering in his heart for a long time. Looking at his pale, sorrowful face, I felt a sudden tenderness tug at my heart.

As soon as he left, I looked up his records to learn his family background. Both his parents were university graduates: his father was an accountant and his mother was a housewife. He also had an older brother. I thought of asking his parents to come to school for a meeting, but quickly changed my mind and decided to wait till the parent-teacher meetings due to take place the following week.

I met his mother at the meeting. She was in her forties but looked years younger because of her fashionably styled, straight hair and well-tailored lilac dress. An aggressive light shone brightly in her big, round eyes, and strings of words seemed to fill her wide mouth, ready to burst through at any moment.

Once she opened her mouth, there was no stopping her. "They're both my boys, but they're as different as night and day," she said. "Yu Zhou's brother is only two years older, but he's better at everything. After the Primary School Leaving Examination, he was admitted into his secondary school's Gifted Education Programme, and remained top in his class. He excels in whatever he does and is most impressive. But Yu Zhou is another story altogether. He can't do anything right. Just think, his brother attends a well-known, top-tier school, while he tested into this average secondary school. What a loss of face!"

With a stern look, I replied, "Mrs. Pang, even one's ten fingers aren't the same length, and here we have two completely different people. To be sure, going to a well-known school shows a student's ability, but it's no loss of face to attend an average school. In fact, Yu Zhou is quite talented. His homework is never late and he's a sensible, responsible boy. It's just that he lacks confidence and gets anxious easily. He seems unhappy."

"Unhappy?" Her voice became shrill and urgent. "He eats well, dresses well, has a comfortable life and is never short of spending money. How could he be unhappy?"

"My sense is that for kids his age, material comfort may not be the most important thing in life." I tried to be tactful. "What they need most from their parents is caring and fair treatment."

"Humph." She sniggered. "He has whatever his brother has. Isn't that fair enough?"

What could I say? This was truly a case of a scholar not being able to reason with a soldier. I decided to help Yu Zhou build up his confidence instead.

A few days later, I showed him a blown-up photograph that made his eyes shine with puzzlement. He was quiet for a while before asking, "Is that a cat?"

I nodded. It was a photo I had taken the year before while I was travelling in Myanmar. I'd heard about a temple on scenic Inle Lake where they kept cats with special skills, even though scientific research has shown that cats cannot be trained. After a long, exhausting journey, I finally found the temple and told a monk my purpose for visiting. Without hesitation, he whistled, drawing one, two, then three, and eventually over a dozen cats out of various nooks and crannies. The cats stood in a neat row before us. The monk held a rattan hoop high and called out in Burmese, "Jump!" Seeing was indeed believing, for one cat took the lead and without hesitation, it leaped unerringly through the hoop. The other cats followed suit, jumping again and again with apparently high spirits. Not a single one missed. Later in my conversation with the monk, I learned a touching anecdote related to the unusual cats. There was once an abbot who had spent thirty-nine years alone in the temple with cats as his only companions. As someone who believed that faith and willpower could conquer any difficulty, the abbot began training newborn kittens, trying to turn the impossible into the possible. First he put the rattan hoop on the ground for the kittens to crawl through. Then he slowly raised the hoop little by little, day after day, month after month, and year after year. Years went by and the hoop was gradually raised until he finally succeeded in getting the cats to jump through the hoop. An unusual phenomenon occurred. When the kittens saw the older cats jump, they believed they could do it too and so, without much effort, they learned to jump easily through the hoop as well. People from neighbouring villages heard about the cats and sent their own to the temple, but strangely these outside cats never learned to jump, no matter how long they stayed at the temple or how often they watched the temple cats jump. The reason was quite simple. Since the day they were born, the temple cats had seen the older cats jump, so they thought they were born to jump. With no psychological block, they learned naturally, while the village cats could not because they were not prepared mentally and lacked faith.

As I told Yu Zhou the story in great detail, he listened with rapt attention, a bright light shining in his eyes. Not letting up, I continued, "Remember, Yu Zhou, heaven helps those who help themselves. You have to depend on yourself if you are to show your true worth."

In life's long journey, we often unconsciously lock ourselves in dark, sunless corners where we suffer alone. However, a well-intentioned and well-planned conversation can sometimes turn things around. I hoped that what I had told Yu Zhou would have the same effect.

2

Our school was organising a funfair to hone the students' ability to work independently. They were to pool their money together for a commercial enterprise and on a particular date, stalls would be set up on campus for games or the sale of food. After deducting the money spent on materials, whatever the students made would be added to their class fund.

I divided the thirty-odd students in my class into three groups: one would be responsible for setting up the stall, one would take charge of publicity and one would coordinate.

I also made a daring decision. I wanted Yu Zhou to be the leader of the first group in charge of stall setup. When I mentioned it to him, however, he responded with his usual dubious, uncertain look and turned me down.

"I can't, Madam Tham. I'll mess it up."

"Yu Zhou, if you say that before you've even started, you've already suffered psychological defeat. Didn't you make a wish to reach any goal and accomplish anything you set your mind to?"

With his head bowed low, he revealed his hidden worries. "The other students won't listen to me."

"Don't worry. I will help you convince them," I said, patting the back of his hand.

It was not an easy task—everyone in his group objected. I tried appealing to them with emotion and persuading them with reason. I did this many times until they finally consented. In private I also met with Teo Rui Qi, a well-liked student in class, and told him frankly about Yu Zhou's situation. After hearing my plan, Rui Qi nodded and readily agreed.

"Please don't worry, Madam Tham," he said. "I'll help him out."

I was in attendance when Yu Zhou held the first meeting. It didn't start out well. He was so nervous that his face turned bright red and he couldn't articulate his thoughts. Some of his classmates began to whisper among themselves, others sniggered, while some simply turned to look out the window. Then Yu Zhou took out a box of chocolate with nuts, everyone's favourite candy, and placed it on the table. He stammered, "Here, please, have some, everyone. Just to thank you for your help."

Everyone stared at the box of chocolates wrapped in shiny gold foil and turned to look at one another. Things were getting awkward. I was about to say something to smooth the situation over when Rui Qi spoke up. "Put the chocolates away, Yu Zhou," he said. "We'll work together. First we need to decide what we want to do—a food stall or game booth?"

Once Rui Qi spoke up, the atmosphere in the room quickly went from freezing to boiling point. Now everyone was talking at once. In the end, the class made a unanimous decision to run a food stall at the funfair.

Yu Zhou, who had been a bundle of nerves, began to relax and even made a suggestion about what to sell. "There's a coffee shop near my house," he said. "Their otak-otaks are very good. I can order them."

Otak-otaks are traditional cakes in Singapore made of fish and shrimp paste mixed with coconut milk and spices. Wrapped in banana leaves, they are slowly baked until their aroma becomes irresistible. Yu Zhou's idea was quickly accepted. The students also decided to sell other food such as fried chicken wings, fish balls and fried rice, each under the charge of individual students.

The students began to work in earnest. Like a snail sticking its head out of its shell for the first time, Yu Zhou was dazzled by the outside world. At first he was fearful and timorous, and the pressure turned his bony face thin and pointed like a shoehorn. But little by little, through frequent contact, the other students got to know him better, and they felt his sincerity more keenly. His behaviour was still immature in many respects, and his ideas were not always well thought out, but his classmates' attitude towards him was visibly different. Their disdain was gone. Sometimes they even joked with him and he would smile shyly, looking quite happy.

With full cooperation and participation from everyone, the preparations for the funfair were soon complete. During this period of eager anticipation, no one suspected that a particularly outrageous and shameful incident was about to occur.

Shortly after the principal had commenced festivities at the funfair, the school was swarming with visitors. Parents, friends and relatives of the students all came to show their support. I went to check on the stalls early in the morning to make sure nothing was amiss. The students were creative and had decorated their stall beautifully. The smooth, round fish balls were so plump and enticing that no one could pass them up. The golden fried chicken wings looked as if they might take flight with the people's fancy. The fried rice resembled a large plate of sparkling jewels. The rice looked like pearls; the sliced carrots, red rubies; the snap peas, emeralds; the sliced eggs, thin gold filigree. The two hundred otak-otaks were piled high, and their alluring aroma lingered in the air.

Visitors crowded around the stall to buy the otak-otaks. Some bought five, some bought ten, twenty, thirty, and others, many more. As the pile shrank, the students congratulated Yu Zhou on his foresight. He smiled happily, showing his sparkling, porcelain-white teeth. It dawned on me how nice he looked when he smiled.

Just as everyone was cheerfully making sales, a spine-tingling scream sounded not too far away. Before we knew what was happening, a woman had raced up to our stall. Bam. She slapped a partially eaten otak-otak on the table, yelling and screaming with terror.

"There are worms in this otak-otak! How dare you sell stuff like this?"

Everyone's eyes were now fixed on the same spot and more onlookers crowded around. It took just one look to make people retch. One after another, fat, white maggots were crawling merrily in and out of the otak-otak. I grabbed it and dumped it into a plastic container intended for the fried rice, before taking the woman aside and apologising profusely. I said and did all I could to appease her, short of bowing and scraping. We had purchased the otak-otaks from a coffee shop, but were ultimately responsible for the condition of the food and should have checked it beforehand. Other customers soon found maggots in their otak-otaks as well, and came back to return them. Some even cursed us loudly, which drew an increasingly large crowd. Without hesitation, I told the students to collect everything and to shut down the stall to avoid angering any more customers.

The fiasco resulted in a lot of wasted effort and a huge loss of capital for us. There were other problems as well. The school intervened to investigate, and Yu Zhou was questioned. Then the administration sent someone to deliver the remaining otak-otaks to the Consumers Association of Singapore to report on the shop that had sold us the otak-otaks.

I knew that Yu Zhou felt bad, but so much was going on that day that I was unable to find the time to speak to him. The next day, he didn't come to school. When I called his house, I learned from his mother's tiresome chatter that he wasn't feeling well.

"You see, what did I tell you? Even though he's incapable of doing anything, he still wanted to participate in the activity. See what's happened? Now he's turned into an ostrich, afraid to go to school. If this had been his brother, it would have turned out different—"

Unfortunately I had no earplugs to block out the non-stop crackle of verbal firecrackers, so I had to rudely interrupt her. "Can I see him?" I asked.

"Don't," she replied at lightning speed. "He's not really sick. He'll be back in school tomorrow. He's just a worthless kid who can't do anything right."

At that moment, I felt that Yu Zhou was like a piece of pottery. He looked fine on the outside but was crisscrossed with internal cracks that put him on the point of imminent breakage, all because of a mother who was like a series of minor tremors. I hoped to be the super glue that would keep the pottery whole.

He came to class the next day with a sallow, grey face and eyes that were glazed over. His head drooped when he saw me.

"I'm so sorry, Madam Tham," he mumbled.

I looked at him and said gently, "Listen, Yu Zhou. I never thought it was your fault. When you do something, you give it your all, but after you do your best and something out of your control happens, that doesn't mean you're incompetent." I paused and continued, "Remember the cat, Yu Zhou?"

"What cat?" He looked up listlessly.

"The hoop-jumping cat."

He nodded eagerly.

"Before it could jump through a small rattan loop, it must have suffered thousands of setbacks. Do you lack the courage and determination of a cat?"

A faint smile appeared at the corners of his mouth, which had once been drawn down by gravity's pull.

A month later, the school was plunged into intense preparatory work for our thirtieth Founder's Day celebration, and I called Yu Zhou to the staff room.

"Yu Zhou," I said, "I'm going to form three preparatory units in our class. Would you like to lead one of them?"

This time he hesitated only briefly before saying, "I'll give it a try."

A beautiful glow of anticipation shone on his face.

PART TWO

Sensitive, Fragile Hearts

An Orchid in Bloom

1

ALTHOUGH IT HAS been many years, I still cannot forget the shock and puzzlement caused by Xi Lan Hua the first time I saw her.

It was the first day of the new school year and my first day teaching at this secondary school. I was to serve as form teacher of Secondary 5D, a class in the Normal Stream, which followed a five-year, less intensive curriculum.

Roster in hand, I took attendance. Of the thirty students, all but one responded to the roll call—that student was Xi Lan Hua. I was about to note her absence when the patter of footsteps sounded outside the classroom. Someone was chasing someone else. Accompanying the noisy footsteps was a string of expletives, but most shocking of all was that the unending vulgarity came in the crisp, clear voice of a girl. Dashing into the room, she was panting hard, yet she somehow managed to let off another string of venomous curses, eliciting gleeful, ear-splitting laughter from the boys who had been chasing her. Although late to a class for which the teacher was already standing in the room, she did not so much as greet me. Instead she shook her shoulder-length hair nonchalantly, headed for her seat, and threw herself down in the chair she'd dragged out from under her desk. Then she caught hold of a length of hair and twisted it around her fingers. Her big eyes, with their sharply contrasting blacks and whites, looked sideways at me, displaying disdain and cynicism. Strangely, the other students seemed so accustomed to her unusual behaviour that no one showed a hint of surprise or disgust. Rather, they strained to suppress smiles as they watched inquisitively to see how I would react.

I looked quietly into the pretty face, which was brimming with rebellion, as I thought fast. Should I ignore her vulgar outburst? No, that would make me an irresponsible teacher. Should I pretend that I didn't see her ill-mannered display? No, that would mar my dignity as a teacher. But reproaching her on the first day of class was likely to only make matters worse. If provoked, who knew how a caustic girl like her might react?

I quickly settled on a strategy. Calmly I called out, "Lan Hua!" I addressed her by her first name, which was an uncommon practice among strangers, and this came as a surprise to her. Lan Hua's defiant eyes now took on the look of a police dog: watchful, cold and pointed.

"I don't have an invisibility cloak, you know, Lan Hua," I said.

She stared at me suspiciously for a while before finally responding, "What does that have to do with me?"

"Why did you pretend I was transparent and not greet me?"

The other students giggled, which made Lan Hua relax, and invested her face with something approaching a smile. "Madam Tham," she called out perfunctorily.

"You have a pretty name," I continued off-handedly. "Did you know that *lanhua*, the orchid, is Singapore's national flower?"

"Not true," she retorted smugly. "Singapore's national flower is *hujihua*."

"*Hujihua* is a transliteration of the English word, orchid, which in Chinese is *lanhua*. You have such a pretty face and elegant name. How lucky you are!"

Thinking I would scold her, Lan Hua's face reddened in response to this unexpected public praise. With the animosity in her eyes gone, she was prettier than ever.

I turned to speak to the whole class. "As a matter of fact, all your names come from your parents' deliberate efforts, and these names usually have profound meanings. Maybe one day I can explain your names if there's time."

That got the students so interested that they were relentless in their desire to have the meanings of their names explained. Seeing that I'd successfully diverted their attention from Lan Hua, I beat a hasty retreat.

"All right, all right. In the future, I'll explain one name each day."

Then I opened the outline for that year's curriculum to give the class a brief description, followed by a detailed explanation of school rules, as well as guidelines on awards and punishments, before concluding with student appearance.

"At your age, all you need to do is maintain a clean appearance and you'll be fine." I intentionally glanced at Lan Hua as I continued, "Being clean refers not only to your outward appearance, but to your language as well."

At that, her large eyes moved away from my face to look out the window. She remained silent and indifferent.

2

Madam Khoo, who taught mathematics, had been Lan Hua's form teacher the year before. When I brought up Lan Hua's name, she reacted with a look of contempt.

"Orchid flower? She should be called 'Odious Flower'. She's incorrigible. I've given up on her. To tell you the truth, she's got no shame. If you scold her, she pretends that you're serenading her. Give her a demerit point, and it's like making a musical notation. So in the end, I treated her vulgarities as nothing more than farting."

I was taken aback by Madam Khoo's harsh words. When she saw a worm-infested apple, she preferred to toss it away instead of trying to remove the worm. Wasn't this contrary to all the principles of education?

I looked at Lan Hua's school record to better understand her family background. The word "Labourer" had been entered in the column under "Father's Occupation" and my heart ached when I saw the word "Deceased" under the column for "Mother".

Ah, she was a motherless child.

I called her father, Xi Ya Fu and asked him to see me the following day, regardless of how busy he might be.

"What for?" he asked in a coarse voice.

"I want to talk to you about your daughter, but please don't tell her I called."

"Lan Hua?" Anxiety was now discernible in his voice. "What's she done?"

"We'll talk about it when you get here, all right?"

"Aiya, what's the matter anyway?" he exclaimed, letting out a string of expletives.

Now it was my turn to be dazed.

Lan Hua's father came early the next day. He looked exactly the way he sounded. Brawny and coarse, he was a heavy-set man with high cheekbones who had the nasty look of a troublemaker. A tattoo of a soaring dragon adorned each of his arms, which seemed to have been moulded out of iron. Highly animated and energetic, his arms, his mouth, everything, moved when he spoke.

I tried speaking to him in a mild tone. "Mr. Xi, Lan Hua is a girl who likes to use vulgar language in class. It's a bad habit, and I hope—"

Amazingly, before I had even finished, a torrent of familiar swear words rolled smoothly out of his mouth. The hint of a smile danced across his swarthy face.

"That crazy girl. I've told her nobody likes a vulgar girl, but she won't listen to me. What can I do? Her mother died when she was young, and I have to work. I can't watch her all day long. You're her teacher, so help me make her change. She's the only child I've got, so I let her do what she wants, I can't be too strict. No kids these days listen to you. But this girl of mine isn't so bad. She doesn't steal and she doesn't rob people, so using a few swear words doesn't seem like too big a deal."

It was depressing listening to him. I felt like a scholar trying to reason with a soldier. There's a saying that goes, "A dragon begets a dragon, a phoenix begets a phoenix, and the offspring of a mouse only knows how to burrow". It might have been a cliché, but it was true. Mr. Xi had been a successful role model and raised a queen of vulgarity. Clearly I would have to fight the battle alone if there was any way to get her to change.

Over the days that followed, I observed Lan Hua closely. I hoped that by getting to know her better, we could form a trusting relationship and that my attempts to change her would succeed with less effort.

What surprised me was that the other students never considered the vulgar Lan Hua a clown. On the contrary, she was well-liked and everyone seemed to enjoy her company. At times when she was unable to answer a question, other students would find a way, open or veiled, to help her out. When the bell rang, I would often see several of her classmates gathered around her desk, talking and laughing with her.

She turned out to be less rebellious than I had initially thought. Around strangers, she was a human porcupine, trying to keep people at a distance with her erect quills, when in fact she was afraid of being hurt. As long as the other person showed a willingness to be friendly, however, her animosity quickly vanished. I could not put my finger on it, but somehow she gave me the impression that she was very insecure, and that there was a dark shadow deep down inside, which she tried to cover up with a devil-may-care attitude.

I regularly made a point of commenting on her good looks in front of others. In fact, she was a very pretty girl, with thick brows and large eyes under long, curly lashes, and a face with chiselled features that gave her a modern look. Best of all, she had two barely visible dimples, which added a reserved elegance to her untamed beauty. When she opened her mouth, however, her looks were spoiled by the vulgar words that peppered her speech.

I called her into my office and sincerely shared my observations with her. She reacted by rubbing her cheeks and asking incredulously, "I'm pretty? Really? You think I'm pretty?"

"Hasn't anyone ever told you that before?" I asked with a smile.

"Everyone calls me a tomboy," she replied honestly.

I laughed and said, "Well, your beauty is overshadowed by the vulgar words you use."

"I've been using those words since I was young. It's hard to change." She sounded resigned.

"Give it a try, Lan Hua," I urged her. "I'll help you. We'll work on it together. You're such a pretty girl, it would be a shame to let your language ruin that."

She gazed at me with her large, bright eyes. She really was pretty—when she was quiet, that is.

I tried my best to find an appropriate remedy for this stubborn illness that had plagued her all these years. It was clear that neither restraining her with school rules nor using morality as a standard would work. All girls want to look pretty, however, so I thought I would be able to achieve the desired result by repeatedly telling her how vulgar language detracted from her lovely appearance.

Starting that day, I walked up to her and asked softly, "Have you broken the rules today, Lan Hua?"

Sometimes she would answer happily, "No, not a single swear word." Sometimes she would giggle and lower her head. I would respond by saying, "Watch out, swear words can ruin your teeth. You don't want to be toothless, do you?"

She laughed loudly when she realised that it sounded like "ruthless".

3

One day I walked into the classroom and heard Lan Hua screeching at a girl named Soh Xiao Ping.

"How could you be so stingy?" she yelled, cursing at the girl.

"I don't have any money. What am I supposed to donate?" Xiao Ping replied timidly.

Bam! Lan Hua slammed her fist on the desk and erupted, "No money? I don't believe you! You paid over three hundred dollars for a branded bag, but can't spare a few dollars to help others. Are you a girl or the devil?"

A student whistled in warning when he saw me standing at the door, sending everyone rushing back to their seats. Lan Hua was still fuming, her face as dark as an ink stone.

I asked the class monitor, Low Zhong Chu, to fill me in on what had happened. One of the girls in class, Teo Wen Xia, was being raised by her mother because her father had passed away when she was young. Her mother, who worked as a cleaning lady, had fallen from a building while cleaning windows the day before and was now in critical condition. Lan Hua had started collecting donations to help out, and while everyone in the class had chipped in, Xiao Ping had refused. That was the reason why Lan Hua was so upset.

When I looked at the list of donors, I was shocked to see that Lan Hua had donated five hundred dollars, whereas the other students had each donated only a few dollars.

I asked Lan Hua to see me after class.

"Lan Hua," I said gently. "I'm touched by your eagerness to help others in need, but good deeds should be carried out voluntarily. Xiao Ping may not have donated due to some personal difficulty, and you shouldn't force her."

"Personal difficulty? Da—"I quickly held my finger to my lips, which stopped Lan Hua from cursing. "She's a selfish, stingy girl with no sympathy for others. I swore at her because I find that disgusting."

"Doesn't swearing at her reflect badly on you too?" I decided not to be too delicate with her, and was surprised when she apologised despite her seething anger.

"I'm sorry," she said.

Recalling the amount of her donation, I said softly, "Lan Hua, you should help others according to your own ability. Your father works hard. Won't giving away five hundred dollars of his hard-earned money cause hardship at home?"

She looked up at me and blurted out, "It's not hard-earned money, it's dirty money."

I was so startled that I just stared at her. Looking as if she didn't care, she told me everything.

"You know, Madam Tham, I really hate him sometimes. He has no sympathy for anyone. He's a hatchet man for loan sharks. When I was a kid, he took me to some of the borrowers' houses, and I saw him use terrible means to force them to pay up."

"What terrible means?"

"Like spraying their doors with pig's blood, or pouring super glue into their keyholes, or writing graffiti on their walls. Sometimes he even splashed faeces and urine into their houses. Disgusting. If the borrower still didn't pay up, he would return with other men to beat him up." A film of tears misted her eyes as she spoke. "Every time someone asks me what my father does, I have trouble answering. It makes me so mad, Madam Tham."

I kept quiet to allow her to vent some more.

"My mum died when I was little and he brought me up. My father spoils me, lets me do anything I want. But when I ask him to stop working for the loan sharks, he says, 'What will we eat if I quit? How will we pay for your tuition?' He gives me pocket money, and of course it's great to have an allowance, but I know where it comes from and spending it makes me feel bad. Madam Tham, I'm so conflicted. Now Wen Xia's mother is in the hospital and I feel like I'm paying for my father's sins by donating five hundred dollars." She stopped, and when she spoke again, she said in an unusually tender voice, "Wen Xia grew up in a single-parent home and so did I. I know how it feels to be lonely. Now she might lose the only person she has, and there's nothing we can do except help out financially. I'm so worried about her."

"Don't worry, Lan Hua. I'll tell the Student Welfare Group about Wen Xia's situation, and we'll organise a campus-wide fundraiser. Your gift is too large, why don't you take some—"

She interrupted me loudly. "Please, Madam Tham, let me fulfil my wish."

The principal made an announcement during the weekly assembly the day after Wen Xia's mother passed away. The students had responded to the donation drive enthusiastically, raising nearly ten thousand dollars. Lan Hua's donation was by far the largest single donation. The Student Welfare Group held a meeting and decided to commend her. In front of the whole school, the principal awarded her with a Certificate for Heartfelt Giving.

To my surprise, however, she didn't seem happy about the award. She came to see me after class that day.

"I don't want the award, Madam Tham," she said glumly.

"Why? What's wrong?"

"Others will think I worked so hard because I wanted this."

I laughed and gave her a big hug.

"Silly girl. This is what you deserve, not what you sought to get. There's no need to worry. Our school motto is to reward the good and punish the bad." Suddenly I hit upon an idea. "Would you like to join the Prefectorial Board and help the school out?"

Her eyes lit up, but the light quickly went out.

"They have such stringent criteria. They'll never take me."

"I'll speak up on your behalf if you're interested."

She nodded quietly, barely able to suppress the happiness in her eyes.

It turned out to be much harder than I'd thought to make her a prefect. Most of the teachers were against it, for they had no faith in her and frowned upon her constant use of foul language. One of them, Madam Kok, even commented disdainfully, "With her on the Prefectorial Board, I'm afraid we'll have to change the name to the 'Cursing Board'."

Somewhat unhappily, I said, "As educators, aren't we supposed to open our arms to all? What would happen to our mission if we gave up on a student, and took opportunities away from her simply because she had some issues?"

With a snigger, Madam Kok replied, "All right, if we agree to give her a chance and make her a prefect, can you guarantee that she will stop swearing, that she will work hard, and that she won't have a negative influence on the other prefects?"

She was relentless with her aggressive challenges, but I was unfazed.

"No guarantees, but I'm happy to try. And I believe that Lan Hua would want to try too. Why don't we give her a one-month trial period?"

A sardonic and provocative smile emerged on Madam Kok's face.

"You seem so confident, why stop at a trial period? Why not grant her lifetime membership? Wouldn't that be better?"

"A trial period is needed even with highly experienced teachers like yourself, so doesn't it seem logical that a young, immature girl like Lan Hua would need the same?" I answered coolly.

Madam Kok's face reddened. She was so tongue-tied that she could only glare at me.

After school that day, Lan Hua and I had a frank conversation in the school's garden. I told her that I had given the school a bold promise, and asked her to accept the challenge. She didn't say anything for a long time. She just looked at me, the expression on her face displaying the myriad of emotions she was feeling: doleful, thoughtful, grateful.

"I won't let you down, Madam Tham," she finally said. "Don't worry."

I had been right. Once she put on the green and white tie that represented her new status, Lan Hua carried herself altogether differently than before. As others' views of her began to change, she redoubled her efforts and was determined to turn over a new leaf. The more outstandingly she performed her duties, the more applause she won. A positive cycle had been formed.

Watching her transformation, I was reminded of a true story that had taken place in Morocco. Every September, young girls of marriageable age gather at a bridal market for single men to choose from. After a man has picked out a girl, he discusses the purchase with her family, in front of her. The least expensive girls cost one camel, while others are purchased with the number of camels commensurate with their attributes. One young man made a fortune doing business away from home before returning to marry his childhood sweetheart with the most valuable gifts and goods. The girl was so homely that one camel would have sufficed to earn her parents' consent. Hence the young man became the town's laughingstock. No one, however, could have anticipated that she would undergo a dramatic transformation. The love and respect of her husband instilled in her face a glow that dazzled anyone who looked at her, and she became well-known in her town for her exquisite and ingenious handicraft. Now people marvelled at the good fortune of the wealthy merchant. What had he done to deserve such an outstanding woman for a wife?

Lan Hua was just like that Moroccan girl. No one had discovered, let alone affirmed, her inner worth, which had caused her to have such low self-esteem and self-pity that she had given up on herself.

Now that someone had given her respect and the chance to show what she was capable of, she transformed from an annoying, cawing crow into a magnificent and graceful peacock. She could proudly display her splendid fan, each bright feather a testament to her impressive accomplishments.

She graduated from secondary school with flying colours and was accepted into a polytechnic where she majored in Information Technology.

During her first three years in polytechnic, she came to see me every Teacher's Day with a large bouquet of orchids. It was impossible to tell which was prettier: the bright flowers or her beautiful face. She found a job in a bank after finishing her three-year course, and was so busy with work that she was no longer able to visit me.

One day, I was in the Central Business District taking care of some errands when I happened to pass by the bank where Lan Hua worked. I decided to go in and see her. She was helping a client enter data into the computer. Her long hair was combed nicely and neatly, and when she pursed her lips, confidence and fortitude shone on her face. After the data was entered, she gave a clear, detailed explanation to the client, who then thanked her profusely. She watched with a smile as the client left, and when she turned, her gaze landed on me.

"Madam Tham!" she exclaimed, pleasantly surprised.

"Lan Hua," I whispered with a smile. "Are you still breaking rules?"

"Madam Tham!" She laughed, a pair of red clouds colouring her cheeks.

She truly looked like an orchid, dazzling in full bloom.

The Wounded Grotto

1

IT WAS AWARDS day and the school was abuzz with merriment, like a blown-up balloon that might pop at any moment.

At seven thirty in the morning, the students filed into the auditorium and sat down in their assigned seats. As the velvet curtain was rising, a tardy student dashed into the auditorium. One look told me it was Che Jia Mei, a girl in my class, but a second look brought on a migraine. Around her neck, she had tied a fashionable scarf which was loud and completely out of place, even from a distance. I then saw Mr. Chew Jian Li, the discipline master, stride over to Jia Mei. Judging by their unhappy expressions, I could tell that they were arguing. It was not long before Mr. Chew reached out to snatch the scarf from Jia Mei's neck, as she quickly jerked her head away from him. She was no match for Mr. Chew, however, who swooped down and removed the scarf with hands like a hawk's talons. Fast as lightning, Jia Mei raised her right hand, and with the whole school looking on, gave Mr. Chew a savage slap across the face. The auditorium burst into an uproar, and chaos ensued.

The school administration formed an ad hoc disciplinary committee to deal with the incident, which shook the school. As Jia Mei's form teacher, naturally I was a member of the committee.

Being tardy and wearing a scarf were both violations of school rules, but slapping a teacher topped it all. She wouldn't be able to talk her way out of this with a million excuses, especially since she had worn the scarf to cover love bites on her neck. The fiercely intelligent Jia Mei, however, managed to complicate what should have been a black-and-white affair.

At the hearing, she argued eloquently in a measured voice. "Of course it was wrong to slap him, but he's a male teacher, and when he reached out to tug at my clothes in public, how was I supposed to know what he was thinking? I slapped him out of self-defence."

Self-defence, she said! Mr. Chew's face turned purple. Assaulting a teacher was an inexcusable offence, but on the other hand, the Ministry of Education had clearly stipulated that a teacher was under no circumstances to touch a student. This obviously put Mr. Chew at the losing end of the dispute.

After a series of administrative meetings, a decision was made to speak to Jia Mei's parents and to give Jia Mei a major demerit point. In addition, Jia Mei was required to make a public apology to Mr. Chew. But that wasn't the end of it. The bruises on her neck indicated she was in a romantic relationship, which was strongly discouraged by the school. I was asked to look into the matter and give the girl some guidance.

It was turning into an impossibly thorny case.

2

Jia Mei was a loner on campus. She wore her hair short around an oval face, and she had the dark, changeable eyes of a cat—sometimes limpid and sparkling, at other times misty and glassy. Most of the time, however, daggers seemed to be hidden in her eyes. They gave off a gloomy glint as if she was about to attack. Just looking into her eyes made one shudder. Frankly speaking, it was rare for a fifteen-year-old girl to be so cynical and misanthropic. She had no friends, and the other girls wrote her off as being narcissistic, while the boys just thought she was too proud. No one wanted to be her friend. She enjoyed being alone, coming and going as she pleased and ignoring everyone else. Usually she was like a silent goat with sharp horns, but she posed no danger so long as people gave her a wide berth. Yet, if provoked or if she sensed a violation of her personal privacy or interest, she would turn into a fierce lion—quick to pounce, viciously and relentlessly attacking until her opponent was left torn and bleeding.

I recall an incident where two girls had been gossiping about Jia Mei outside the toilet stall she was using, and she had heard every word. Without any preamble, she stormed out of the toilet stall and nearly beat them unconscious.

The discipline master was called in to resolve the incident, and that was when I gained first-hand knowledge of her incredible ability to argue a case. She spoke calmly and her words were convincing.

"I know it was wrong to hit them, but they were spreading rumours with the power to hurt me. Isn't that worse than hitting someone? Ask them what they said. I don't believe anyone can stand that kind of talk. Giving them a couple of slaps was merely helping the school to teach them a lesson."

So the discipline master asked the girls exactly what unsavoury things they had said. But they hemmed and hawed, unwilling to repeat their own words, which only added wind to Jia Mei's sails.

"Hearing such filthy words would make you sick," she remarked coolly. "Who knows how many more students would have fallen victim to their vicious slander if I hadn't taught them a lesson today?"

In the end, the discipline master put the three girls in a small room to reflect on what they had done and apologise to one another. After a day, the two girls wrote heartfelt apologies, but Jia Mei would not accept them, and she refused to apologise for assaulting the girls. Instead she acted as if she had carried out a sacred deed. "When you hit someone, you're always in the wrong, no matter how many good reasons you think you have for doing it," I said, trying to talk some sense into her. "So why not admit you were wrong and put an end to the matter?" But she maintained that she was right, and stubbornly refused to apologise. Ultimately she received a minor demerit point on her record. Her obstinate nature left an indelible impression on me.

Later I spoke to the two girls in private and learned what they had said:

A: Hey, I'll let you in on a huge secret. Yesterday I saw Che Jia Mei at a shopping centre. She was going into the cinema with her boyfriend, arm in arm, looking very intimate.

B: Really? The way she acts at school, eyes staring straight ahead, you'd think she was Joan of Arc reincarnate.

A: Humph. The loftier some people look on the outside, the more lewd their behaviour. Sometimes they pretend to be aloof and haughty to cover up their shameful activities.

B: You're right. I hear that some girls have clients off campus, like part-time work, you know. Maybe Jia Mei is one of—

That was when Jia Mei stormed out to slap them. They were awful things to say about another girl at school, and now that I had learned the truth, I sympathised with Jia Mei. On the other hand, I still thought she needed to reflect upon her view that she was always right and others were wrong. So I talked to her often, advising her to treat the school as one big family and to mingle with others. But she would simply shrug and coolly respond, "To each her own." Later when I thought about her comment, I had to agree that over one's long journey through life, everyone has the right to live how one prefers. Besides, as the Chinese philosopher Zhuangzi once said, "You're not a fish, so how do you know that a fish is not happy?" Why should I meddle in other people's affairs? So I let her be, never imagining that this loner would stir up so much trouble as to make herself the most notorious person on campus.

3

It turned out that Jia Mei had a fairly simple family background. Her father had died of a heart attack when she was in primary school and she lived with her mother in a semi-detached house in Katong. I had met her mother, Ms. Sng, several times.

I was surprised by her mother's good looks the first time we met. She had fair skin with the gentle, soft lustre of jade and a smooth, wrinkle-free forehead. Her short, curly hair was dyed a fashionable brunette. Her light green, leaf-shaped earrings swayed when she spoke, emitting waves of sparkling emerald green light, which gave her an unspoken charm.

She was visibly apprehensive when Jia Mei's name came up. Unconsciously, she reached for the purse on her knees with one hand and fiddled with it the whole time. When she spoke, she sounded insincere, phony even.

"She's a good girl," Ms. Sng said. "I have no problems with her at home."

"She's not very sociable. In fact, she's a loner. It's unusual for a girl her age to prefer being alone," I said. "Also, she's somewhat prone to violent behaviour. What do you think could be the cause?"

"Ah, I really don't know what it could be, she's a good girl at home."

She kept saying that Jia Mei was a good girl. Obviously she was being deliberately protective of her daughter, insisting that everything was fine. Frankly, she was the kind of mother a teacher dreads most. I noticed, however, that Jia Mei treated her with impatience and indifference. She was often annoyed with her mother, and rude most of all. When her mother spoke to her, Jia Mei either responded gruffly or completely ignored her. I couldn't help but sigh over the fact that mothers like her usually ended up with unruly children. As a single parent, she was probably doubling her love to make up to her fatherless daughter for her sorrow and emptiness. Often it is precisely this tendency to overcompensate that inadvertently results in another form of regret.

After our initial encounter, I saw Jia Mei's mother again at several parent-teacher meetings. Each time she gave the impression that everything was fine, that nothing was out of the ordinary and that there was no bad news. Finally I couldn't hold back any longer and asked pointedly, "Ms. Sng, don't you think that Jia Mei has a somewhat distant relationship with you?"

That caught her by surprise and she froze. It took her a while to reply, "Uh, um, in the past, it wasn't like this in the past."

"She always seems rude to you. Why is that?"

She lowered her head and began to play with her purse again. After a long silence, she said haltingly, "I remarried the year she was in secondary one. It's been hard for her to accept."

"Ah, so you've remarried." Now I was the one caught by surprise.

I recalled how Jia Mei had always written "Deceased" in the column for "Father". When a new form was filled out each year, she continued with the same information: "Deceased".

"My late husband died when she was only seven and I was barely twenty-eight. I was so lonely that when I met someone suitable seven years later, I married him. After all that time with only each other for company, Jia Mei couldn't accept the change in our life and she still hasn't forgiven me. I'd thought she'd get used to it after a while, but it's been three years and she has yet to utter a single word to her stepfather. It's difficult being caught in the middle. Can you help me, Madam Tham?"

As the saying goes, one cold day does not lead to three feet of ice. Jia Mei's mother hadn't tried to break the ice when it was forming and now that the floe had turned into an iceberg, she was asking for help. It truly felt as if she was hoping the rice would still be raw even after it was cooked and ready to serve.

I mulled over the matter and said, "I'll see if I can talk her around."

In order not to ruin my chances of success, I decided not to say anything just yet. Instead I waited quietly for the right moment.

4

Father's Day was soon upon us. In class, I guided the students in a discussion of the meaning of Father's Day, and to tie the discussion to their study of the Chinese language, I asked them each to come up with a creative metaphor to describe their fathers.

After careful consideration, the students let their imagination take wing.

"My father is like an encyclopedia. He knows everything."

"My father is like an ocean. He has the capacity for anything."

"My father is like a bottle of white-out. He helps us correct all our mistakes."

"My father is like bread. He fills our stomachs with food so we don't go hungry."

"My father is like the roof. He shelters the family from wind and rain."

"My father's words are like a popular song with a pretty melody. You never tire of listening to it."

"My father is like an ATM. He'll give you whatever you want."

"My father is like a web page. He'll give you all the information you need."

"My father is like an alarm clock, lending his help at the right moment."

"My father is like glue, binding the whole family tightly together."

"My father is like Mickey Mouse. Everyone loves him."

These metaphors were rich in imagination, conveying fresh, new images that greatly amused the students. They could not stop laughing as they described their fathers and listened to others do so as well.

When it was Jia Mei's turn, she kept her mouth tightly shut. After repeated urging from me, she finally replied icily, "I don't have a father. He's long dead."

Another student raised his hand, and with a maturity beyond his years, said quietly, "My father is dead too, but to my mother and me, he's still alive. He'll never die." He continued in a highly emotional tone, "If I were to use a metaphor, I'd say my father is like air. You can't see him but he's everywhere."

That earned loud applause from the class. I stole a glance at Jia Mei, but she looked utterly unmoved. She remained indifferent and nonchalant.

After class, I said to her, "Come with me, Jia Mei. I'd like to speak with you."

I took her to an open, grassy area in the rear of the campus. The field was trimmed so nicely that it resembled a perfectly woven carpet. Trees blanketed the area beyond the fence, and the sky behind the trees was so clear it seemed as if the clouds had been brushed off it.

We sat side by side. The early morning air was as refreshing as sparkling clear spring water cascading down the hills. Birds were singing, their chirps a continuous song in our ears.

I got straight to the point. "Jia Mei, you seem very unhappy."

She turned to face me. "You're right," she said frankly. Then she looked up at the sky before blurting out, "I want to be a bird in my next life."

A bird. I chuckled softly. The sky may be vast, but even it cannot contain all the worries of birds. The birds know how treacherous the sky can be and every bird, like every human, has its own troubles.

But I decided to follow her train of thought.

"A while ago, I had two birds. They were so happy they were always singing. But then one of them died, and the other became so aggrieved that it stopped eating and drinking. It got to the point where it was probably going to die, until someone advised me to get another bird. So I bought another one to keep it company. Now they have each other and they are both happy." I paused and fixed my gaze on her. "You see, Jia Mei, even a bird needs company, let alone a human being."

She cleverly saw through my thinly veiled intent. Anger mounted in her eyes as she said rudely, "Did my mother ask you to speak on her behalf?"

I tried to reason with her calmly. "Jia Mei, peace in a family makes everyone happy. If you accepted your stepfather, you'd spare your mother the pain of being stuck between…"

That was when she lost it and began to scream, "What stepfather? Who says he's my stepfather? He's just my mother's despicable lover. All he cares about is her money. After he got involved with her, he moved into our house and got a share of everything we have. He's a leech. My mother and I were doing fine when we had each other, but now that man has ruined everything. Everything!"

She was screaming. Her tears fell like raindrops.

I was shocked to see how badly she had been hurt. We adults were being too tough on her, accusing her of magnifying her sorrows and worries. No one even noticed that she had become badly twisted in the mould of unhappiness.

I could only heave a sigh. The sounds of the chirping birds suddenly began to get on my nerves.

The next day, Ms. Sng came to the school at my request and I told her what Jia Mei had said to me. Her eyes were as big as cowbells, brimming with shock and incomprehension. She kept shaking her head.

"It's not like that," she mumbled. "To be honest with you, Madam Tham, I've known Jia Mei's stepfather for many years. After my husband's death, my life was plunged into a void that was difficult to adjust to. For several years, I played the stock market and won quite a bit of money at first. Then I began to take risks. I put in more and more money, and I was up to my neck in the market. Then the economy bottomed out, and I was seriously burned. Not only did

I lose all our savings, I was about to lose the house. Zhi Qun, Jia Mei's stepfather, suggested that he buy the house at market value and then lend us the place so we could continue to live in comfort. That arrangement went on for over two years until Jia Mei entered secondary school and I accepted Zhi Qun's proposal, as I thought she was old enough to understand things. She knows all this. So why would she tell you such a different story? In fact, Zhi Qun has always treated her like his own daughter, but she won't have any of it."

Now I was the one who didn't know what to do. If Jia Mei knew the truth, yet chose to tell a lie, then perhaps what she needed was therapy. We had a school therapist, Liew Wen Jia, who provided troubled students with counselling, and I suggested to Ms. Sng that Jia Mei speak with her. As if she had been introduced to a saviour, Ms. Sng nodded repeatedly to show her consent.

After a two-hour talk with Jia Mei, Wen Jia told me that she was the personification of a stubborn mule. She had formed many erroneous preconceptions that seemed so right to her, even a chisel could not chip them away. For instance, she continued to compare, albeit subconsciously, her birth father with her stepfather, and had reached the unshakeable conclusion that her stepfather was inferior in every respect. Her contempt for him was fueled by her jealousy over her belief that he was taking her mother away from her. Gradually, her complex feelings had turned into a hatred that was beyond her control. It would be impossible to eliminate the hatred within a short period of time because it was like ice which had formed over a thousand years, thick and hard. On the other hand, it was better late than never for her to start therapy, because although Jia Mei was suffering from a stubborn, chronic illness, it wasn't terminal and there was hope for a cure.

No one could have predicted that while Wen Jia and I were working on a way to chase away the demon in Jia Mei's heart, another incident would shake the campus yet again. Before one fire could be put out, another flared up, one stunning incident on the heels of the first, like a string of exclamation marks. Everyone at school was speechless and wide-eyed.

Jia Mei had gone to the police station to accuse her stepfather of molesting her, using the bruises on her neck as proof. Her accusation had led to his arrest. Now I understood the Chinese saying that even the best judge is unable to deal with family affairs. I had thought she was merely too immature to accept her mother's second marriage, but it was finally clear that she hated her stepfather for a reason. It seemed possible that he had molested her many times before and that this time he had to own up to it because of the bruises on her neck. I lost sleep over the painful fact that a sixteen-year-old girl had to endure so much suffering. She was too young to go through so much. I blamed myself. Why hadn't I discovered the root of the problem earlier and lent her a hand in time?

5

The incident developed in ways beyond anyone's wildest imagination. It was like watching a movie with a series of dramatic climaxes, so shocking that the viewers sat breathlessly on the edge of their seats.

After a thorough investigation and interrogation, the police concluded without a doubt that Jia Mei had made up the charges. It was another dramatic turn of events. From the accuser, Jia Mei became the accused. Since she was still underage, she was sentenced to a year in a reformative training centre for teenage girls.

By attempting to send her stepfather to jail with false evidence, Jia Mei naïvely believed that she could easily remove the thorn in her side and return to the old days with her mother. But her seemingly clever scheme had backfired, and she had to suffer the consequences.

I went to see her at the reformative training centre. Sitting in the visitor's lounge, she had lost her calm, indifferent façade. Her lips quivered like dead leaves in the wind and tears streamed down her face. She did not say a word, and all I could do was clasp her hands and encourage her to look to the future.

As I was leaving, I ran into her mother and stepfather at the entrance. That was the first time I had seen him. He was not tall to begin with, and looked even shorter because he was overweight, with a round belly like a pea in a pod. He had dark, rough-looking skin which resembled a newly ploughed field. A trusting smile adorned his wide mouth, which gave him the appearance of a well-fed farmer. Only his full head of naturally wavy hair added a hint of tenderness to his untamed look.

His stepdaughter's unfounded accusation had gotten him into trouble, but he didn't let it bother him. Instead he accompanied his wife to visit Jia Mei, armed with bags of food and books. When they saw me, the couple rushed up with grateful smiles. I hurriedly waved away any socially required politeness.

"Let's all do our best to help her stand up again," I said.

The next time I went to visit Jia Mei, I brought her a colourful poster from New Zealand.

"What's this, Jia Mei?"

She glanced at me and said with a hint of impatience, "Isn't that a grotto?"

"Do you know how a grotto is formed?"

She shook her head icily.

"A grotto is made of limestone, which is a soluble rock. After years of erosion caused by water, or more precisely, the carbon dioxide in the water, and with the effects of sedimentation, these strange shapes appear on the limestone surface. Take a look. Isn't this a pretty grotto?" She nodded.

Erosion from acidic water and the passing of time had turned the seemingly indestructible limestone surface into a celestial palace filled with beautiful views, with thousands of charming stalactites hanging down and transforming into wondrous sights. They looked magnificent, so gorgeous and alluring.

"Listen, Jia Mei. A grotto starts out in a primitive and rough state. If a grotto was sentient, it would have screamed and cursed when the acidic water began to erode it. After a long, long time, however, the eroded grotto transforms itself into a stunning beauty." I stopped and said emphatically but slowly, "We're the same. We're like grottos. When an unforeseen disaster falls on us like acidic water, we're hurt. Maybe we become resentful, maybe we complain, and maybe we even feel we'd rather die. But the disaster is there to toughen us up and help us mature so we can display a different yet beautiful appearance."

She looked at me pensively.

I left her the poster, which she carefully pasted over the head of her bed.

6

I made an agreement with the director of the reformative training centre to allow four of our students to take turns visiting the centre to serve as Jia Mei's tutors.

Jia Mei, who thought she had been abandoned by the world, reacted with gratitude when she found herself bathed in so much friendship. The irony was that her boyfriend, who had been so close to her, vanished without a trace after she had entered the centre. Undoubtedly his disappearance was a major blow, but her parents redoubled their care and concern for her. Her stepfather, in particular, treated the disastrous incident as a turning point in her life and showered her with all his love during his frequent visits. His open-mindedness and concern slowly melted the barrier in her heart.

One day I brought along a dictionary for Jia Mei. She gave it back after one glance and said with a smile, "My father brought me a dictionary last week. It's the same as this one."

Ah, she had said "my father" with a gentle and serene look on her face.

I found myself tearing up.

Bruising from Love and Hate

WHEN THE DISCIPLINE master, Mr. Woo Zheng Lu, brought the suspect he had nabbed after a day's investigation to me, I felt a chill rise from the soles of my feet and bore into my heart, which was searing with anger. Speechless, I stared in disbelief at the boy before me.

"Madam Tham," Mr. Woo fumed. "This is the punk who scratched your car. Shall I call the police?"

The sun was a glowing red ball at the edge of the sky when I had left the staff room the day before. As I reached the school's carpark, the ponderous sunset erupted, painting the sky with dazzling colours, and the whole scene resembled exploding fireworks. I watched the sky as I walked, filled with appreciation for the wonders of nature. When I neared my car, however, a pain shot through my heart as if I'd been stung by a venomous insect. The pain spread through my heart like overgrown weeds. Someone had turned my car, which I had bought only the month before, into a canvas for graffiti. The person had left a jumble of scratch marks, which resembled the spreading tentacles of a domineering octopus.

The word "shock" could hardly describe my feelings at that moment.

This was a first in my many years as a teacher. I had never reprimanded or punished my students without sufficient reason.

Whenever any of my students committed an offence, I would talk myself hoarse trying to help that student see the light, while giving him or her a chance to repent and turn over a new leaf. Only the stubborn ones who refused to change would receive a measured degree of punishment from me. If it came to that, I would give them a detailed explanation before the punishment so that they would understand why they deserved it. I have always been a firm believer in winning people over with kindness, so I have never had an unpleasant confrontation with a student. And yet, there was obviously one student who loathed me so much that he had unleashed his hatred on my car, which had suffered serious damage.

Now the culprit was standing right in front of me. Hands in his pockets, he stared ahead indifferently as if the incident had nothing to do with him. When our eyes met, the daggers in his gloomy eyes were hurled viciously at me.

I was reminded of our first meeting nine months earlier.

Secondary 4A was a model class on campus, with diligent, hard-working students who never violated the school rules. Khoo Fan Feng was the sole exception. His hair was cut very short to expose his pale ears. He was always squinting in class and his eyes seemed to wander absent-mindedly out of this world. His gaze, like his face, was hollow and anaemic. Whenever I called his name, however, his expressionless eyes would undergo an instant transformation. They would become watchful like those of a police dog on high alert, filled with animosity. He had built an impregnable fortress around himself and would not, or could not, allow anyone to get close. In class he was like a square peg in a round hole, or a layer of oil floating on the surface of water. As his form teacher, I tried chatting with him several times, but each time he would answer my questions simply with a nod or shake of his head, as if his every word were a valuable gold nugget.

My biggest headache was his tardiness.

When I asked him why he was often late, he clammed up, closing his thin lips so tightly that they formed a short, straight line. According to the school rules, after a student has been late three times, he must stay behind after school to do cleaning chores. What puzzled me was his willingness to stay behind every time I told him to—and he did a good job as well. We never had to check his work. The desks and chairs would be wiped sparkling clean, and the trash on the grass would be removed, returning the school field to its lovely emerald green. When he finished his chores, he would slowly and methodically wash his hands before dragging his tall, thin frame towards the MRT station under the fading light of the golden sunset. But how heavy his footsteps seemed, as if he had been shackled.

His mother was a housewife. I had called a number of times, asking her to see me at school, but incredibly she had missed the appointment three times in a row. Even though I had wasted valuable time waiting for her, she would give no explanation each time, let alone an apology. So I switched tactics, and began trying to get hold of his father instead. However, each time I called Mr. Khoo's office, his secretary would inform me that he was out of the country. Hence school had been in session for several months, but I had yet to meet either of his parents. What exactly was Fan Feng's family like?

I was curious, but no matter how hard I tried, he was a hard nut to crack. In my years of teaching, I have always believed that with enough effort even a steel cudgel can be worn down to the size of a needle. Rome wasn't built in a day. In addition to love, transforming a problem student requires patience and perseverance, and it won't work if even one of those elements is missing. Therefore, ignoring his reactions, I made sure to find time to greet him every day with a few words and a smile. Sometimes I would say "Fan Feng, you did a great job on the last test, so keep it up" or "Fan Feng, you used several of my favourite idioms in your essay this time." When there was nothing special to say, I'd try "Fan Feng, you look great today" or "Fan Feng, you've got dark circles under your eyes. Don't stay up too late." I wanted him to know that he was not an island, ignored and neglected by everyone. I also wanted him to know that I would be his driftwood any time he needed help.

At first I got no reaction, just a wooden expression. As the days went by, however, I saw his taut face soften a little, and as more time passed, he began to nod at me whenever I walked by. More importantly, the animosity in his eyes gradually disappeared. But he was still late for class—that hadn't changed.

One day I was grading the students' exam papers in the staff room when the class monitor ran in, ashen-faced and panting hard.

"Madam Tham, Madam Tham, Fan Feng has been hurt!"

Startled, I leaped to my feet and asked urgently, "How? How did he get hurt?"

"He fell while playing basketball and sprained his ankle. He's lying on the court and his PE teacher told me to tell you."

Fan Feng was still lying on the ground when I got there, his face twisted from the pain. The physical education teacher, Foo Zhi Yu, who was squatting by him with an anxious look, stood up the moment he saw me.

"Madam Tham, I want to take him to the hospital but he won't let me. He says he'd rather die than go to the hospital. Could you notify his parents so we know what they'd like us to do?"

Fan Feng, who was grimacing from the pain, said, "Madam Tham, I don't want to go to the government hospital, but I don't mind a private clinic."

I looked down and was surprised to see his eyes pleading with me. They seemed to be struggling painfully in desperation. I felt a searing pain in my heart.

Then I made a snap decision.

"Mr. Foo, I'll take him to a nearby clinic and I'll transfer him to a hospital if the doctor there thinks it's necessary."

"No, I don't want to go to a hospital," Fan Feng protested.

He was so insistent—something else had to be going on.

I drove rapidly down the street towards the neighbourhood clinic. He rested his head against the back of the seat. His pale face was now a chalky grey.

"Fan Feng, does it hurt really badly?" I asked. He was silent, so I added, "I hope it isn't serious." Still there was no sound from him. After a while, he spoke up in a surprisingly child-like way. "Do I have to take my clothes off during the examination?"

I turned to glance at him when we stopped at a traffic light. He sat up and rolled up his shirt to expose his belly. "Look, Madam Tham." I nearly cried out in shock. His fair belly was covered in bruises—inky black, dark brown, bright red and dark blue—as if he'd been branded by the devil. "My mum did it," he said in a pained voice, as if he'd been seared by a hot iron. "I don't want the doctor to see them. He might report it to the police and my mum might end up in jail." He became quiet again after struggling to tuck his shirt inside his pants. A raging, savage pain rose up from a spot deep in my heart. It was too much to bear and my vision turned blurry.

He held onto his clothes tightly the whole time we were at the clinic. After performing a careful examination, the doctor determined that the injury wasn't serious and bandaged Fan Feng's foot. He prepared some medicine and wrote out a medical certificate granting Fan Feng two days' absence from school, before sending us off.

Since Fan Feng's fears hadn't materialised and his injury wasn't serious, he felt well enough to walk on his own without my help as we left the clinic.

I spotted a fast food restaurant shortly after we got out.

"Hungry?" I asked.

He nodded, so we went in. I ordered a set meal with many items for Fan Feng, which he wolfed down. Clearly he was starving. He gnawed clean several large pieces of fried chicken in no time.

"What do you normally have for dinner at home?" I asked casually.

He glanced up at me. "Instant noodles."

"Every day?" I asked, surprised and uncertain that I'd heard him correctly.

He nodded and shrugged, before adding indifferently, "There are many different flavours. I don't eat the same one every day so I don't get tired of them."

"Doesn't your mother cook?" I probed.

He was quiet and lowered his gaze for a while before saying, "Mum isn't always in the best mental state."

"Why doesn't she go to see a doctor?"

"She suffers from depression," he said glumly. "She's usually fine, but she acts up when my dad goes on business trips. When that happens, she often pinches me savagely. Sometimes I wake up in the middle of the night due to the sharp pain. She pinches me so hard and it hurts so much that it sometimes feels like my whole body is breaking into pieces. Sometimes the pinching goes on all night, till three or four in the morning before I can go back to sleep. That's why I'm often late for school."

"Why doesn't your dad do something about it?" I was stunned.

He began to laugh silently, a sudden, bleak laugh. After a while, he said, "Dad? He doesn't have time for us. He's the one who caused mom's illness in the first place. He's having an affair and goes to see his mistress when he's on his business trips. Sometimes he finds an excuse to go abroad just so he can see her."

Ai! He was only sixteen, yet already suffering physical pain and mental anguish caused by the adult world's tangled web of emotional affairs.

"Listen, Fan Feng," I said, looking very serious. "There are medications that can take care of depression. You're made of flesh and blood, and you can't let your mother torment you like this forever. When I take you home, I'll talk to her and urge her to see a psychiatrist, what do you think?"

He immediately objected. "No, absolutely not. It'll crush my mum if she knows I've revealed our family affairs to outsiders. Madam Tham, please, don't ever tell anyone, please?"

I nodded gravely. "Don't worry," I said. "I won't if you say so."

He stirred the melting ice that remained in his drink with a straw, which made a clinking sound. It almost sounded as if the sobs he had been holding back were now coming from his glass.

"To tell you the truth, Madam Tham, sometimes I really hate my mum. I hate her so much, so much that, um—"He hesitated before letting it out. "That I feel like stabbing her with a knife. But,

but I know how bad she feels inside. We were a happy family before Dad started his affair. Mum was fine then, really she was a great mother who'd do anything for me. Now she suffers so much, and there's nothing I can do to share her pain. So when she pinches me or whips me, even burns me with a red hot spoon as if she were crazy, I can only grit my teeth and put up with it. If hurting me lessens her pain, then I can take it." Tears seemed to drip from his voice.

That day as I watched him limp his way home, the tears in his voice turned to rain in my heart.

I racked my brain, trying to come up with a way to lend a helping hand. But before I could think of a good idea, this shocking and outrageous incident with the graffiti occurred.

Looking at the enraged face that was struggling to look indifferent, I said calmly, "I need an acceptable explanation, Fan Feng."

Mr. Woo cut in angrily, "I think he should give his explanation at the police station."

I turned to Mr. Woo and said, "May I have a moment alone with him?"

Mr. Woo took me aside and gave me a well-intentioned warning. "Be careful, you're dealing with a violent student here."

"It's all right," I said, "I can handle it."

We went out to sit on a stone bench. The dying rays of sunshine felt gentle as they streamed down through the emerald green leaves, giving Fan Feng's face a dark green cast, like the glaze in thousand-year-old moss.

I looked at him, but he turned his head away. "You're not a child any more, Fan Feng," I said. "So please don't be impulsive. I want to know what I did wrong."

It felt like a century had passed before he finally forced these words out: "You're a hypocrite. You don't deserve my respect or my trust."

I was speechless. Where, exactly where, had that come from?

Holding back my temper, I kept up my questions until he finally spoke up in an angry voice filled with loathing. "Why did you tell other teachers about me? Didn't you promise never to mention this to anyone? Why didn't you keep your promise? I steer clear of everyone at school because I don't want them to know about my family, so why did you go around telling people?"

I was in a daze. When had I said anything to anyone? I prided myself on keeping my promises, and I had kept a tight lid on his family affairs.

"You didn't?" He was shouting now. "Yesterday didn't you tell Madam Teo Li Fen? I overheard you when I went to the office to get something."

Teo Li Fen? I stared at him in bewilderment as I searched my memory, but my recollections were like beads from a broken string. I struggled to collect the pieces and string them back together. Finally I found the thread and the sequence. Now I recalled exactly how the conversation had gone. Madam Teo and I had been talking about corporal punishment when I said to her, "He's not a child any more, but his mother beats him black and blue. I tell you, honestly, sometimes I feel like calling the police to teach his mother a lesson. But if she's jailed, he'll be alone since there's no one else to care for him." Madam Teo sighed in a show of sympathy and said, "It's rare for a mother to be so mean." The person I'd been referring to was another boy, who happened to be in a similar situation as Fan Feng. I never thought that Fan Feng would be so sensitive as to presume I'd been talking about him.

I explained this to Fan Feng but he continued to pull a long face, assuming that I was covering up a lie.

"Come, get in the car," I said with a sigh.

"Where are we going?" he demanded with hostility.

"To see the person I was talking about."

He got into the car that had suffered such terrible scratches by his hand. I could tell from his expression that he wanted to see how I would play out the act.

The person I was referring to helped his mother sell chicken rice at a hawker centre. He was mentally disabled, and because of this, his mother used him as a punching bag. She often pinched him here and there until his arms looked as if they'd been painted on. When Fan Feng saw the young boy's colourful arms, he looked as if he had been struck by lightning. His face quickly drained of colour.

He was quiet and kept his head bowed as we climbed into the car after leaving the hawker centre. When I pulled up outside his building, he didn't move.

"We're here," I announced.

That prompted him to look up. His face was bright red from the strain of trying not to cry.

"I'm sorry," he said, his lips quivering. "I wasn't thinking. You can punish me. Do whatever you think is right. I feel terrible and deserve to be punished."

I turned to look at him. "Listen to me, Fan Feng. You made three big mistakes. First, you took other people's words out of context and got yourself into trouble—you were really asking for it. Second, before you checked things out, you acted rashly. Third, you damaged other people's property to vent your own anger. You've made mistakes and must face the consequences. The discipline master will have to deal with your mistakes formally tomorrow."

He kept nodding as if that were the only way to lessen his feelings of guilt. I took a card from my purse and handed it to him before he got out of the car.

"Here's a card for a psychiatrist who specialises in mental and psychological health issues. Take your mother to see him if you really want to help her."

When he took the card, he finally lost his grip on his self-control and a large tear rolled down his face.

Love Fool

DEAR MAILBOX,

Hi, how are you?

Let me tell you a secret. I'm in love.

Her name is Lau Li Fei, a student in Secondary 4D. At school, she's every boy's dream girl, but I'm the lucky one. Over the past year, I'd written her countless letters but received no response. It was like throwing rocks into the ocean. But last week I got my first reply. It was a short letter, only two lines, thanking me for writing her so many letters, which are enough to compile an anthology. Holding her letter in my hands, I read it over and over, savouring every word. For the first time in my life, I realised that words can brim with sweetness. After laminating the letter, I put it under my pillow and when I sleep on it, I am so relaxed that I can almost feel my soul drifting out of my body. Ah, I want to write poetry for her, but I want even more to write a song for her. She's the only person in the whole world who's good enough for my poetry and music. I tossed and turned in bed last night. Someone once said that the heart of a person in love for the first time is like a jar with five spices.

The myriad emotions are like the five tastes of sweet, salty, sour, bitter and spicy. That is no exaggeration.

Wish me luck, Dear Mailbox.
Fong Wei Wen

Fong Wei Wen was a student of mine in Secondary 4C.

I had created this virtual mailbox for the students in the hopes that having such an outlet for their writing would boost their interest in studying Chinese. I asked them to write to the mailbox once a week. Their letters could be long or short and about anything at all. They could openly discuss any difficulties they encountered in their studies or in their daily life, and the "mailbox" would try to find a solution for them.

Students loved the idea and were inspired to write. What surprised me most was that some of the more reticent students wrote lengthy letters to the mailbox, in which they shared secrets they would not otherwise have revealed. As for me, the mailbox moderator, I tried not to preach when I responded to their letters, and steadfastly kept my promise not to share their secrets. I strove to be the students' friend and wrote heartfelt letters in response to each of them. Eventually the more I gained their trust, the more secrets they shared with me.

As I looked at Wei Wen's letter, I thought long and hard of a suitable response. This was clearly going to be a tricky letter.

Young love is a common issue among students in Singapore. Even if they have no desire to be in a relationship, teenagers are sometimes under a certain degree of peer pressure when their friends are all on the lookout for a significant other. A student once said to me, "Three good friends of mine all have girlfriends at school.

I don't want to fall in love so early, but they often tease me as being gay. It's really upsetting." Even amongst those who had found "the one", there were some who were not prepared for long-term commitment. "It's just for fun," they would say indifferently. "We'll stick together as long as we can and when we can't, we'll break up. There's no need to be too serious."

Most surprising to me was the fact that Wei Wen had been working hard with the single-minded purpose of going to university; yet he had fallen for a popular girl known as the school flower. Even more surprisingly, Li Fei had actually responded to his letter.

They were ill-matched in every respect. Wei Wen was an outgoing boy, bright and sunny, who did well in school. He was well-liked by everyone, good at sports and talented in literature and music. For Teacher's Day the year before, he had composed a song and sung it onstage with his guitar, captivating everyone at school, teachers and students alike. Li Fei, also a student of mine, was pretty with exceptionally fair skin and dark, thick hair. She also had large, lively eyes, as well as nicely round, charming dimples. This pretty girl was haughty and arrogant, however, and had a bad temper. Like a porcupine, she would often hurt the feelings of many boys who tried to get close to her. It is human nature to want to be near beauty, so despite her ill treatment, many boys continued to pursue her with the fearless attitude of moths flying towards a flame. The harder it was to be with her, the crazier the boys got.

Although there were several versions of her family background being circulated around the school, it was in fact quite simple. She was born into a wealthy family. Her father was the general manager of a multinational corporation and her mother was the chairwoman of a charitable organisation. As their only child, it was easy to imagine how she was always allowed to have her way. I was concerned that a naïve boy like Wei Wen would not be able to deal with a picky girl like her who was hard to please. Besides, the secondary four students were facing a critical end-of-year exam, and any romantic distraction would surely affect their performance. At this crucial point in time, however, I couldn't possibly feed him the usual platitudes, for I knew very well that he would never share his secrets with me if I poured cold water on his dreams.

After prolonged deliberation, I decided on a subtle approach.

Wei Wen,

It is natural for young people in their late teens to feel the attraction of the opposite sex. But you should keep in mind that instant noodles are far less nutritious than porridge, which has been slowly cooked for hours. A relationship developed over time will last a long while without losing its potency, whereas a romance that is hurried into fruition may wither quickly and die. So don't be too anxious to see it fulfilled, and let time be the soil for love to grow.

Best wishes,
Dear Mailbox

Wei Wen had become a different person. He was so absentminded in class that I would often have to call his name several times before he would respond to my questions. His school work suffered too, and he was no longer as conscientious as before. He had also stopped playing basketball with his friends after class. Instead he shut himself up in a corner of the room, where he buried his head in scribbling. I supposed he was writing poems for the girl he admired. Li Fei, on the other hand, was the same—haughty and aloof. Instinct told me it was unrequited love on Wei Wen's part. What puzzled me was that if Li Fei wasn't interested in seeing the relationship bloom, why had she planted the seed of love in his mind?

Wei Wen's anguish soon overflowed into his letters.

Dear Mailbox,

Our Chinese language teacher gave us a fun exercise last year. She asked everyone to find a vivid and apt metaphor for love. After we had thought long and hard, all sorts of ingenious and interesting metaphors were offered: love was like a sunset, coffee, fine wine, chocolate, the sun, the moon, the stars, lemon, spring flowers, winter snow, mint, waves, poetry, sugar, pepper, the list goes on. Someone's comparison of love to a person's buttocks, since both are so mysterious, put the finishing touch on the exercise. Everyone was eager to know what that mystery might be, but since it was an awkward topic, we were left disappointed. For me at this moment, however, love is like nothing other than the goldthread herb, which has only one taste—bitter.

Dear Mailbox, I want to tell you something that has been heartbreakingly painful for me. One day Li Fei agreed to meet me at a fast food restaurant on Holland Road. I went there filled with excitement, but after waiting half an hour, I was surprised when she strolled in with six friends. They ordered so much food that I nearly ran out of money to pay for it. It was really embarrassing. At that moment I felt like

I'd been had. It wasn't about the money though, it was just that I felt things seemed to be moving in a strange direction. Over this past week, she's only spoken to me twice—once in the hallway and another time at the school entrance—and both times because she'd wanted me to photocopy my notes for her. Dear Mailbox, to tell you the truth, I'd be happy to do anything for her, but for some reason I feel like she's using me. Am I being paranoid? Am I? Each time I try to catch her eye, I bump up against an icy look in return. On the other hand, love is like poison. I'd gladly drink it if it could quench my thirst, and let what happens happen.

When we said goodbye at the restaurant that day, her beautiful smile made me feel as though I were standing on a mountaintop. I wrote her a poem and put it to music after I got home. I hope to play and sing it for her, but will she be willing to give me a chance?

Fong Wei Wen

Ah, those who are caught in the middle are often befuddled, and only a bystander can see clearly. It was obvious to me why Li Fei had agreed to be with Wei Wen—she was simply using him to embellish her vanity. How could such a smart boy be so foolish?

I wrote him a story.

Wei Wen,

On the surface, love looks like a beautiful rainbow.
Love can be an enchanting game, but it can just as easily turn into entrapment.

True love, on the other hand, is a long-term promise to share the good and the bad. Care and respect are the two most important elements in love. A melon taken by force will not taste sweet, and forcing someone to love you never works.

Let me tell you a story.

A was an eighteen-year-old boy who was madly in love with B, a girl of the same age. She had no feelings for him, but liked to boast to her friends about the "trophy" she'd gotten so effortlessly. She teased him at every opportunity, but he mistook her actions as positive responses to his courtship. He committed one foolish act after another. One day she asked a few friends over to revise for the exams. At two in the morning when everyone was hungry, she picked up the phone and asked A, who lived twenty kilometres away, to buy food for them at a twenty-four-hour coffee shop. She even told him that instead of ringing the doorbell, he should place the food by the front door so that he wouldn't wake her family. He struggled down the slippery roads on his bike through a thunderstorm, with knife-like lighting flashing and thunder rumbling. The pelting raindrops seemed to stab like arrows and daggers, slicing through his heart. A frenzied pain awakened him, and he realised that a light had gone on in a secret place inside of him. At that moment, he was assaulted by the heartrending agony that accompanied his awakening. At the coffee shop, he bought the steaming food she'd instructed him to get and put each container into a plastic bag. Hanging the bags from his handlebars, he braced himself against increasingly strong gusts of wind which were about to send him flying. Head lowered, he pedalled for what seemed like eternity before finally arriving at her block of flats. He was soaked to the bone, but it might have been tears and not rain that drenched him. He took the elevator to the eighth floor and put the food down outside her entrance. He could hear crisp laughter through the flimsy door. By then, it was already four in the morning. Wiping the water off his face, he stood there silently for a while before turning to leave. As he stepped into the elevator, he knew this would be his last time there. Strangely, though, the pain he felt was followed by a sense of relief, as if he'd shed a great burden. He also experienced the joy of regaining his confidence and dignity.

Dear Wei Wen, if you feel you are being taken advantage of, it is time to re-examine the relationship.

Remember, don't ever be a love fool.
From Dear Mailbox

Silence ensued. For four weeks, Wei Wen did not write a single word to the mailbox. I didn't say anything to him either; I merely watched his every move. He was unusually quiet, as if undergoing the painful process of metamorphosis.

At long last, there was another letter from him one day.

Dear Mailbox,

I experienced the biggest, most severe shock of my life when I read about the love fool.

Yes, shock.

After reading your reply, I felt as if someone had slapped me to wake me up. I tried to rationally analyse this relationship that had yet to really begin and surely had no future, and I realised that you were absolutely right. I was not enjoying the sweetness of love. I was merely being a love fool.

I could put up with her cold shoulder, and didn't mind if she didn't answer my letters or pick up my phone calls, but I simply couldn't accept that she had passed my letters around to her friends, and portrayed me as an unrefined person.

We are like parallel lines that will never cross to produce sparks. I've made up my mind not to be a love fool.

Thank you, Dear Mailbox.
Fong Wei Wen

The Boy with Golden Hair

1

IT WAS AROUND nine in the morning. The sky was a familiar and pleasant azure blue. I was in my car heading to an HDB estate in Redhill in search of the address in my record book. It was 8 August, the eve of Singapore's National Day, and the red and white national flag was proudly displayed in every window. The lively white and bright red colours put the sparkling-diamond sunshine to shame.

Silent excitement percolated through the housing estate, but excitement was a far cry from what I was feeling because I was on an unpleasant mission. I was coming to see a student.

While I was reviewing exam papers in the staff room the day before, Mr. Chiong Mao Yan, who taught physics and was known as "The Firecracker", had stormed in, dragging a tall, skinny boy behind him. Mr. Chiong was barely in the door before he shouted angrily, "Look at this, Madam Tham. Look at this clown from your class."

Before me was the ever reticent Song Li Long.

He was wearing a cap whose elongated bill cast a shadow on his long, narrow face. His glum eyes were trained on his shoes as if they were studded with diamonds.

"Do you know why he wears a cap to school?" Mr. Chiong asked, still fuming.

I stood up and cast a fierce look at the young man, who was a head taller than me. "What did you tell me this morning when I asked you about it, Li Long?" I asked deliberately, enunciating each word.

He refused to answer, so I repeated what he'd told me earlier, word for word. "You said you have head lice, and that the doctor told you to keep your hair clean for a few days. Isn't that why you've been wearing a cap to school?"

Mr. Chiong sniggered.

"Well, those must be powerful lice, since they were able to change his hair colour."

He snatched the cap off the boy's head, and instantly one, two, three, countless jarring golden rays of light shone all around. I was stunned. Oh my God, Li Long had dyed his inky black hair a disagreeable yet eye-catching golden yellow! His gloomy face resembled the sky before a storm, and the yellow hair which now framed it not only clashed but actually looked laughable. Instead of laughing, however, I felt an irrepressible anger rise up inside me.

I have always detested dishonesty. That was why every year I impressed upon my students that regardless of whatever problems they faced, they had to be honest with me. They should never try to hide something or cover it up, and never ever lie. Paper cannot contain a fire and no secret lasts forever. When one lies, one has to lie again to cover up the first lie. It is exhausting for the liar and difficult for others. A wise person would never try it.

Having done just that, Li Long was now standing before me, and I looked like a fool for being sympathetic.

"Why did you lie to me? Explain yourself!" I said in an unusually harsh voice.

The face framed by golden hair remained stubbornly silent. An angry lion makes for a poor conversation partner.

I quickly made up my mind. “Go home and dye your hair back to black,” I said. “Come see me tomorrow morning at seven o’clock.”

He walked off with a lowered head and hunched shoulders. His disappearing back looked burdened with a thousand pounds of rice, whereas I felt the proverbial bucket with its thousand pounds of rice weighing down on my heart.

I couldn’t help but feel that trends are sometimes like drugs. They are powerful lures for teenagers. Those who cannot resist the temptation violate school rules and risk angering their teachers as they become willing slaves to trends. Even someone like Li Long, a quiet student who spoke little and seemed more mature than his classmates, had failed the test.

Obviously unhappy with how I’d dealt with the boy, Mr. Chiong said disapprovingly, “You’re letting him off the hook just like that?”

“He made a mistake,” I said calmly, “and I think we should work to correct the error before we talk about other matters.”

With a sardonic snigger, he continued, “You told him to come see you tomorrow morning. Aren’t you being too easy on him?”

I looked at him with questioning eyes.

“Don’t forget,” he said, “tomorrow is National Day and there are no classes, just a celebration ceremony. Do you think he’ll dye his hair back as you told him to and obediently come see you?”

“I’ll punish him if he doesn’t,” I replied evenly. “He’s in my class, so it’s my responsibility.”

Deep down I was wondering the same thing. Would he keep his promise?

I was on edge.

The next day I got up at the crack of dawn and waited for Li Long at school. Due to the National Day celebration, the campus was festive, with laughter all around. But I couldn't bring myself to be part of the festivities, for I was in the grip of a strong, irrepressible anxiety. Again and again I looked toward the school gate, but again and again I was disappointed—he had not shown up.

By eight o'clock that morning, I knew that Li Long was not coming.

I felt like a defeated soldier, and thought I might explode from the anger building up inside me. That he'd lied was bad enough, but I couldn't forgive him for squandering the chance I'd given him to make amends. I decided I had to do something right away—I would go to his house and personally drag him to the barber, where I could watch his hair return to black with my own eyes.

2

Li Long opened the door, still with a head of shiny, golden hair. Incredulous, he stammered, "You—eh, who are you looking for?"

I fixed my gaze on his shifty eyes. He was apprehensive, obviously knowing he had done something wrong.

"You, of course," I said coldly.

"What for?"

"To see if you've dyed your hair back."

A hoarse voice emerged from inside the house.

"Who's that, Ah Long?"

"It's my teacher."

"Your teacher? Hurry up and invite her in."

Li Long lived in a one-bedroom flat, which was simply and crudely furnished. A few chairs and a table were the extent of the ensemble in the small, cramped living room. An old woman in her seventies was sitting in a rattan chair, her left foot wrapped tightly in a white cast. Her face, crisscrossed with wrinkles, showed signs of painful struggle as she tried to stand up to greet me but knew she couldn't make it. A silent plea settled on her upturned face. She was asking for my forgiveness but at the same time was afraid I couldn't understand her inner turmoil. Hence a myriad of emotions played across her face—a mixture of awkwardness, humility and sadness. She nodded, smiling and gesturing as she repeated, "Please have seat, Madam Tham. Please sit down. Sit. Quick, Ah Long, pour some tea for your teacher."

The long-limbed teenager stood there awkwardly, not knowing what to do. Growing impatient, the old lady looked as if she might throw off her cast, stand up and pour the tea herself.

"The tea, Ah Long," she repeated anxiously.

As if waking from a dream, Li Long raced into the kitchen, his bobbing head creating golden arcs that flickered in the dimly lit room.

"How are you and Li Long related, Granny?"

"Ah, he's my grandson, my only grandson." She swallowed and asked in a concerned voice, "Has he done something bad at school?"

"Li Long is a good student." I was telling the truth. "But for some reason he decided to dye his hair yellow, which is against school rules. Yesterday, I told him to dye it back and he agreed, but he decided to stay home today."

"Dye his hair!" The old woman's wrinkled face twisted in pain. She looked down and said with some difficulty, "I did it for him,

Madam Tham. Please don't be angry with him."

I said nothing. This was another case of a family member blindly spoiling her child. Instead of trying to get to the bottom of the matter, the family member takes the blame since she is out of punishment's reach, not caring how angry the teachers may be, or how strict the school rules are. Love like that, however, is a weighty burden.

"Madam Tham—"When she spoke again, her voice broke. "Please believe me, I did it."

Li Long came out with a cup of freshly brewed tea, and the old lady clammed up. When he set the tea on the table, I noticed a half-finished bowl of porridge.

"Finish your porridge, Grandma," he said softly. "It doesn't taste good cold."

She reached out and patted the back of his hand. "Take it back to the kitchen. I'll eat it later." She paused. "Ah Long, go downstairs to buy a bottle of medicated oil, and while you're at it, deliver the laundered clothes to our three customers."

He looked at me and hesitated. Seeing that he was not moving, the old lady said, "Go on. I'll explain everything to your teacher."

He put three piles of neatly ironed clothes into a large bag and nodded at me before walking out the door.

I turned back to her, but before I could say anything, I was startled to see tears brimming in the old woman's murky eyes. She didn't want me to see her tears, but she couldn't hide them and this made every wrinkle on her face quiver with pain. Although she dried her tears with the back of her hand, they seemed to emerge from her voice instead. "Madam Tham, I'm sure you don't know Ah Long's background. He's a proud child and doesn't want anyone to know. His father, my only child, is a good-for-nothing man who gambles and visits prostitutes. My daughter-in-law, Ah Long's mother, walked out when he was only three, and we haven't heard from her since. That worthless son of mine now lives with another woman and never comes home. I'm raising Ah Long all by myself."

As I listened, Li Long's precocious face kept appearing in my mind's eye.

"During the day, I wash and iron for three families. At night I wash dishes for a nearby restaurant. I make enough to support the two of us. Everything is so expensive these days, and it's tough providing for us and sending him to school. As luck would have it, I fell the other day. Like they say, you're useless when you grow old. Ah Long has always wanted to find an after-school job, but I wouldn't let him. Now we need money for my injured leg, for food and for his tuition. I don't have any savings. Madam Tham, you can imagine how worried I've been." She stopped, put her hand to her chest and coughed a few times before continuing. "A few days ago, some of his friends came to see him. They told him they have a gig at Clarke Quay for the National Day celebration. It will last a month, and they wanted him to join them. The pay is quite good, and the performance is legitimate. Ah Long wanted to do it, so I went along with it. But then they said he had to dye his hair. I thought it would only be for a month, so I bought the dye and did it for him. Madam Tham, please believe me, I didn't know it was against school rules to dye his hair."

I left before Li Long returned. The dancing and singing were still going strong when I got back to school.

3

I went to Clarke Quay that night. The area was swarming with tourists whose bobbing heads turned the place into a sea of humanity. The rippling Singapore River was a splendid sight beneath the ever-changing neon lights, with restaurant after restaurant lining the riverbanks. People crowded into each other amid the mouth-watering aromas of food, creating an unlikely harmony. Noise from the spectators and the din of music merged to fill the quay with sound, smell, colour and light.

In the distance, shafts of light from an elevated stage swept across the area in all directions, resembling bolts of lightning sent down from heaven. Surging crowds turned the stage area into a wall. I struggled, an inch at a time, and exhausted all my strength before finally managing to edge my way to the front.

Six boys with golden hair, wearing identical clothes, were dancing about on the stage and singing. I looked carefully at each of them, but no Li Long. Puzzled and suspicious, I wondered if the old lady had lied to me. Had she and her grandson colluded to deceive a trusting teacher?

I mustered enough patience to watch them sing and dance for twenty minutes, until finally the singers turned hoarse and the dancers were drenched in sweat. They stopped and the MC said, "Now, let's hear it for a pantomime by Ding Ding and Dang Dang!" The crowd erupted with applause, cheers and whistling as if the area were drenched in a sudden downpour. Everyone roared with laughter when Ding Ding and Dang Dang came onstage.

Ding Ding was tall; Dang Dang was short. Ding Ding had yellow hair; Dang Dang's was red. Their faces were colourfully painted, and they were wearing gaudy, loose tops and baggy pants. Unable to suppress their excitement, children cried out, “Clowns! Clowns!”

Without a word, the two clowns began tumbling. The tall, long-limbed clown was particularly agile as he performed a series of neat somersaults, while the clumsy, short one tried to imitate him, only to fail miserably, falling again and again, which elicited cheap laughs from the audience.

Then it struck me—the tall one was Li Long.

Spectators roared with laughter as he performed comical movements. His big mouth, painted blood red, was wide open in an eternal, worry-free smile. I knew, however, that if not for the tough life he lived, this proud young man would never have subjected himself to selling his smile in front of so many people. He pulled out all the stops, but whenever a round of laughter exploded from the crowd, I felt an invisible whip lash me, leaving one burning, painful mark after another on my heart.

Once the performance by Ding Ding and Dang Dang was over, I elbowed my way out of the crowd and headed backstage, where I told the staff watching the area that I needed to talk to Ding Ding.

When Li Long emerged, still wearing his makeup, he was so surprised that he simply froze. His blood-red mouth, painted wide in a happy smile, continued to present a joyful, ignorant face. It was terribly disconcerting.

“Madam Tham,” he murmured.

“When will you be finished, Li Long?” I asked quietly.

“I have one more show to go. I’ll be done at nine.”

“I’ll wait for you at the teh tarik stall by the river after nine o’clock.”

He showed up at a quarter past nine. He had obviously left in a hurry, for his face hadn't been washed clean. Patches of paint remained here and there, resembling colourful tears.

I ordered a teh tarik for him. The Indian stall owner made the tea in the traditional way, which is fast dying out in today's society. He raised one hand high and held the other low. As the raised hand turned and flipped, freshly steeped, steaming tea fell from a tall decanter and was transformed into a slender cascading waterfall, but before the stream reached the ground, it rushed into a small cup held low to receive the liquid. Not a drop escaped, and the cup was filled. But the owner wasn't done yet. He repeated the same show, sending the golden waterfall rising and falling, soaring and flying. It was a beautiful sight.

When the teh tarik was served, Li Long looked down, seemingly absorbed in his tea. He was frowning, however, as if he'd spotted a fly in his glass. I didn't say anything. Some time passed before he said in a low voice, his head still hanging, "I'm sorry, Madam Tham."

"You didn't do anything wrong, Li Long. There's no need to apologise."

He looked up at me, his face overcome with incredulousness.

"You dyed your hair, you lied about it, and then you skipped school. On the surface, you're a misbehaving student who broke school rules. But I must judge you from a different angle and see if you had a good reason to do what you did."

His Adam's apple bobbed but no sound emerged.

"Your biggest mistake was not telling me about your difficult situation. But now, listen, I've asked the school's Student Welfare Group to give you a monthly stipend—"

Before I could finish, he cut in with his usual stubborn look. "Please, Madam Tham, don't. I don't want any help from the school."

So he would rather be a clown in public than receive aid from the school. He clearly had a serious complex. I wanted to help resolve his issue, but no matter how I probed he refused to give me a straight answer. Instead he kept saying, "I want to be self-reliant."

Time ticked away and I was burning with anxiety. That morning, when I had applied for aid with the school's Student Welfare Group, I had some serious explaining to do. The teacher in charge, Goh Sheng Nan, showed me Li Long's record, which listed his parents' occupations.

"Father: construction foreman; mother: housewife." Mr. Goh continued to explain, "Song Li Long is a single child. His father is a construction foreman. It's a profession with quite a good income. We have no reason to give him any money."

I told Mr. Goh about Li Long's family background, but he wanted proof.

"What kind of proof can he produce when his father refuses to come home?" I asked.

"I can't take the student's word for it, I need proof," he said.

"Make a family visit then." I was getting agitated.

"Even if everything checks out, we'll still need a guarantor," he said.

"Guarantor? What for?" I was more than surprised.

"If it turns out to be a scam, then the guarantor will have to pay back all the money."

"I'll be his guarantor. Will that work?" I said, without thinking.

"You don't need to—" He gave me a questioning look, but I cut him off.

"Please give me the required forms."

Even after a prolonged discussion, however, Li Long still refused to accept the financial aid I had applied for on his behalf. Out of frustration, I gave him a piece of my mind. "Listen, Li Long. Your grandma told me that your father likes to gamble and visit brothels. He hasn't been home for a long time, leaving your grandma to raise you. Now she's injured and is worried sick about paying for your tuition. How can you let someone who loves you so much suffer like that?"

"My grandma, she told you everything?" He looked at me. His lips were quivering as a profound sadness slowly seeped into his eyes, which were blurring with tears.

"Madam Tham, I don't want aid because I don't want to end up a parasite like my father. Do you know that he often comes back to ask my grandma for money? She's old but he hits her when she has no money for him. Once he even rammed her head against the wall." His face twisted in pain as he spoke. "Later, when he came, I stood at the door and shouted, 'Don't come in. If you do, I'll call the police.' One time we even got into a fight at the door. The neighbours came and helped me to drive him away. He's absolutely shameless." At that point, tears poured down his face as though a dam had broken. I could almost hear something heavy collapse inside his heart. The pale moonlight turned into a blurry glow in my eyes.

I waited for him to calm down before continuing, "Li Long, your father's shameless demand for money from your grandma is not the same as taking financial aid from the school. We're simply loaning you the money."

"A loan?" He looked up at me with puffy eyes.

"Yes, it's a loan. When you graduate and find a job, you'll repay the school as your financial situation allows." I patted the back of his hand and said with a smile, "At that time, if you can, you can even set up a Song Li Long Scholarship Fund."

It was a starry night. At that moment, a light brighter than the stars shone in his eyes. And I knew that the young man who had backed himself into a corner had finally struggled away from his dark path.

PART THREE

Stumbling Stones on the Path of Study

Eggs Would Smile If They Had Feelings

1

"YOU HAVE A transfer student this year." The administration manager handed me a small stack of documents on the first day of the school year.

The student was a girl named Ong Shan Shan, who was transferring from a nearby secondary school. She had an exceedingly pale face that was so square, it looked like a sheet of neatly cut paper. Her eyes were large and dark but lustreless. They reminded one more of salted fish drying on a riverbank. She was not talkative, and when she did speak, she lowered her eyes as if her words were sparkling gold nuggets, which she was ever-ready to bend down and scoop up. Years of teaching experience told me that something was not quite right about her, but I couldn't pinpoint the problem.

The first day of school is always the busiest, and I was so preoccupied that time passed quickly. After class the school cleaner came to see me, and told me that someone was waiting for me in the reception room.

That someone was a middle-aged man whose wrinkled face looked like a freshly ploughed field, coarse and plain. His short hair was speckled with white, resembling an early frost. Smiling guilelessly, he held a large, rustic-looking paper bag. The moment he saw me, he walked up, displaying profound respect and humility. "How, how are you, Madam Tham?" he stammered.

"You are?"

"Ah—I, I," He swallowed hard and shifted the bag to his left hand, before continuing anxiously, "I'm Ong Shan Shan's father."

"Oh, Shan Shan." I smiled. "She reported to school today."

"Please, Madam Tham. Please watch over her." He looked down and said with a bit of a stutter, "The poor girl. Her mother died shortly after she was born and I raised her all by myself. It hasn't been easy." He paused. "Her health is poor and sometimes she may have to miss classes if she's not feeling well. I hope that won't be a problem." Then he handed me the paper bag. "Just a token of my gratitude. Please, please take it."

I waved my hands and shook my head vigorously, but he showed no sign of backing down. Thrusting the bag at me, he said loudly, "Please, Madam Tham, please take it. These are just eggs, nothing valuable."

Oh, eggs! That stopped me from pushing the bag towards him, for fear that a careless move would crack the eggs and hurt his feelings. I would feel terrible if that happened.

After I'd reluctantly accepted the bag, a happy smile blossomed on his face. Rubbing his thickly callused hands, he nodded and said, "So I'll be off now. Bye, Madam Tham, goodbye."

Inside the bag were ten paper cartons layered on top of one another, each holding ten neatly placed eggs. My God, he had given me a hundred eggs! Was he hoping that his daughter would score a hundred marks in each subject?

I could only smile wryly as I looked down at the one hundred snow-white eggs.

When I got home that day, I decided to make tea eggs. After boiling the eggs, I cracked their shells, poured water into a pot and added the proper amount of soy sauce, sugar, salt, sesame oil, anise seeds, cassia bark and cloves, before placing the eggs in the pot. After an hour, I turned the heat off so the eggs could soak in the mixture of condiments.

The next day I reheated the liquid. The aroma was so strong and enticing that I found myself nearly drooling. When I peeled the eggs, I saw that the dark brown mixture had etched patterns resembling wrinkles onto their snow-white surfaces. They were so beautiful. I brought the eggs to school and shared them with my colleagues, setting aside twenty that I gave Shan Shan to bring home to her father.

Imagine my surprise a few days later when I saw Shan Shan waiting outside my office with another large paper bag. She held it out to me and said shyly, "My father told me to give these eggs to you."

"I can't, Shan Shan," I said gravely. "I can't accept them again. Please take them home."

With an awkward look, she replied, "Pa said you made tea eggs for us and we have to return the favour. Please take them."

Ai, when would it ever end, with eggs coming and going like this? I mulled over the matter and replied, "Wait for me at the gate after school."

She smiled with relief, as she assumed that I'd accepted the eggs. But she lingered after I took the bag and looked at me as if she had more to say.

"Do you have any other questions, Shan Shan?" I asked.

"Madam Tham, the tea eggs were delicious." Her face turned bright red as she struggled to continue. "Could you teach me how to make them?"

"Sure." I laughed. "I'll give you the recipe after school."

A charming light shone in her dull eyes, almost like a miracle, and I suddenly realised that, in fact, Shan Shan was a pretty girl.

She was waiting for me at the gate when school was over.

"Get in, Shan Shan. I'll drive you home."

She showed no expression as she got in. Her family lived in a three-room HDB flat in Clementi and her father ran a small egg stall in Clementi Market.

"How are you adjusting to the school?" I asked as I drove.

She was quiet for a while before finally managing to respond, "I don't know."

"Is there anything I can do for you?"

"I don't know."

We chatted like that along the way, but I got little out of her. When we reached the car park in front of her building, I gave her back the eggs and said gently but firmly, "Please tell your father not to give me any more eggs. I appreciate his intentions, but I can't accept them."

With the bag in hand, she watched me drive away with disappointment written all over her face.

I hadn't expected to see her father waiting at the school gate early the next morning. As soon as he saw me, he bowed and apologised profusely. "I'm sorry, I'm so sorry. I should've brought the eggs myself yesterday," he said. "But I've been so busy recently, I can hardly get away from my stall. Shan Shan must not have said the right thing, which was why you refused the eggs. So I came in person today. I picked every one of these myself. They're fresh."

I tried everything but could not turn him down. Looking at the hundred eggs in the paper bag, I began to feel dizzy. The man before me was as stubborn as a hundred-year-old banyan tree, utterly immovable. But I would soon learn just how stubborn and troublesome he could be when the issue was Shan Shan.

A few days later, when I saw Shan Shan enter the staff room with another paper bag, I felt my scalp tingle. I had developed egg-phobia. She headed straight to my desk and, handing me the bag, said in a mosquito-like voice, “Here are the tea eggs I made, Madam Tham. Try one.”

Tea eggs? How quickly she applied what she had learned! I took the eggs and tried one. I was impressed. In addition to the usual taste, there was a unique, lingering flavour. I asked her what it was.

“I added angelica and Western ginseng to the spice mixture,” she said shyly.

This student had truly outshone her teacher. I gave Shan Shan a thumbs-up, which brought a smile to her face.

2

Shan Shan’s father told me that she had transferred to our school because poor schoolwork had kept her back a year. Not wanting her to feel bad at the same school, he had decided to move her to a new learning environment.

She was quiet and attentive in class and her homework was always neat and on time. But she was of average intelligence. Although she performed acceptably when dealing with straightforward issues, she was lost when we moved on to more complex topics. All her teachers doubled and tripled their efforts to help her, but she failed the exams in many of her subjects.

The only person who could not stop praising her was Ms. Tang Mei Xian, her home economics teacher.

"Shan Shan's creativity and intuition are impressive. For instance, for years I've been using orange-flavoured powder when teaching the class to make orange cakes, but she recommended using fresh orange juice. I tried it and the results were amazing! Also, when I teach students how to make jelly, I've always used canned longan juice. She suggested substituting the juice with dried chrysanthemums cooked in sugar water. I followed her advice and it was delicious. This girl could have a bright future if she chooses cooking as a career."

In March, the school's home economics department held a sandwich-making competition. Naturally Shan Shan represented Secondary 3D. As this was the first contest of its kind, the students were excited about the event.

When I turned up to show my support, I was surprised to see how different the glum, unhappy student in my class was as she prepared food at her table. Bright-eyed and smiling, she carried herself with confidence. For the contest she made a "rainbow sandwich", mixing finely chopped cherries, mangoes and apples with tuna and mayonnaise to create a layered sandwich. Then she added tender greens and bright red tomatoes. She held an edge over the others in presentation alone. After tasting all the entries, the three teacher-judges unanimously voted Shan Shan's creation as the best. She was all smiles, lending her such a charming glow that even I was taken by her indescribable beauty.

I called up Shan Shan's father to schedule an appointment. I told him that I wanted to share some good news. What I really wanted to talk about, however, was Shan Shan's worrisome performance in class.

He came early the next day. I shook his hand.

"Congratulations! Shan Shan won first prize in a contest."

"What? Really?" He beamed and turned to give his daughter a tender glance. "She didn't say anything when she got home yesterday. What kind of contest?"

"A sandwich-making contest—"

His face darkened before I could finish and he said with a frown, "What's the point of winning that kind of contest?"

Shan Shan kept quiet with her head bowed low, as if she had done something wrong.

He went off like a machine gun before I had a chance to say anything.

"I'm uneducated, illiterate, and that's why I spend my life working hard at the market, but not Shan Shan. She has to study because that's the only way for her to have a future. Do you know I've already saved up for her university fees? What kind of future can she have cooking and frying?"

The words rolled out of his mouth like steel pellets, harsh and decisive, with no room for negotiation.

I tried to tell him in a roundabout way that Shan Shan really hadn't done well in her tests, and that her studies would require more attention from him.

"Please find me a tuition teacher, Madam Tham," he replied without hesitation. "I don't care how much it costs, as long as she has help in all her subjects."

Shan Shan, who had been quiet all this time, spoke up in a sad, bleak voice, "Please, Pa, I don't want a tuition teacher."

He turned to look at her and said tenderly, "All right, that's fine. We won't hire a tuition teacher. You just make sure you study hard."

After he left, I told the girl, "Shan Shan, I want to set up an after-class study group. Would you like to join us?"

She hung her head wordlessly for a long time. Her face was tear-streaked when she looked up. "I don't want to study, Madam Tham." She was choking up. "I really don't. No, it's not that I don't want to, I'm just not cut out for it. My father doesn't understand so he keeps pushing me."

"Shan Shan, you're only sixteen. What would you do if you didn't stay in school?"

"I love cooking. I'd like to enrol in a culinary school."

Every trade has its star. She loved cooking and could have a dazzling career if she was willing to work hard at it. The problem was her father, who believed she had to study, and that anything else was beneath her. It would not be easy to persuade him to change his mind.

She came to see me a few times after our conversation, each time with the same request: that I convince her father to let her drop out of school and transfer to a three-year culinary training programme sponsored by the Singapore Hotel Association.

I checked with her other teachers, who shared my view. Shan Shan's academic ability was limited and she didn't enjoy studying, so she would suffer the fate of being held back another year if she stayed on. Everyone agreed that she ought to face reality and make other plans.

After I told him what the other teachers had said, and what Shan Shan herself had in mind, her father replied with steadfast determination, "No way. She has to go to university, she must. She's my only child and I want her to have an easy, comfortable life."

Shan Shan, who was sitting quietly to the side, was biting hard on her lower lip as a film of tears began to mist over her large eyes.

3

May arrived, along with the exams.

All sorts of negative rumours about Shan Shan began to spread on campus. The other students described her in graphic detail, how they had seen her mumbling to herself as she roamed the campus alone, or how she would burst out laughing for no reason. The most vivid description came from the class monitor: "It was after six late one afternoon when I left campus and heard someone sobbing on the stair landing. I went to look, and it was Shan Shan. She was sobbing and rubbing her head with a notebook. It was scary."

I had not witnessed any unusual behaviour from her, but it was obvious to me that she had undergone a drastic change. Her face, which had always been sickly pale, now looked completely drained of blood. She spoke in a monotone, sounding mechanical and lifeless. Whenever her gaze landed on me, I got a creepy feeling as if she were a drifting ghost or an illusory spectre. It broke my heart to see her like that, and I felt myself tearing up inside. She couldn't do well at school, but didn't have the willpower or the heart to go up against her father's good intentions. The giant shadow of the exams looming over her was so oppressive that she was nearing her breaking point.

But what bothered me most was that no matter how much concern and willingness to help I showed, she simply shook her head coldly and indifferently, over and over.

I called her father again to tell him about her situation, but he dismissed it as a sign of her lack of sleep from studying too much and said there was no need for me to be concerned. I tried everything I could to help, but both father and daughter ignored me. As the exams drew closer and work began to pile up, Shan Shan's situation was pushed to the back of my mind.

The exams finally started.

The first exam was in mathematics. When I saw Shan Shan's empty seat, I made an urgent telephone call to her house, but the phone rang endlessly as if it were located in a deserted valley. Just when I was about to explode with anxiety, her father returned my call.

"I'm so sorry, Madam Tham. Shan Shan is in the hospital. While I was taking her to school just now, she fell off the back seat of my motorcycle. It was an accident. Luckily it's not serious. Could you please arrange a make-up exam for her?"

Fell off the back seat of his motorcycle? An accident? For some reason I felt apprehensive. I wondered if she had fallen intentionally in order to avoid the exam. Or could she have given up on living? The thought sent a chill up my spine like a slimy, slithering snake. I snatched my car keys and raced to the hospital.

I was shocked. The sight of Shan Shan in a hospital bed made me suck in cold air. As her father had said, her situation wasn't serious, but what shook me was the look of hopelessness on her face.

Her father was sitting beside her bed with a tormented look. When he saw me, he rubbed his hands together and said, "It was my fault. I should have been more careful. Eh, Madam Tham, eh, have you made arrangements for the make-up exam?"

I signalled to him to step outside so we could talk.

I went straight to the point. "Can't you see that Shan Shan was trying to kill herself?"

"Kill herself?" He was so shocked he was speechless for a while. "How could that be possible?"

"Well, maybe you should get a psychiatrist to see her," I said.

"If she doesn't commit suicide, she'll go crazy due to the unbearable pressure of studying for the exams." I hardened my voice. "You must do something now. I assume you don't want to see this sort of thing happen again."

4

The psychiatrist's diagnosis was that Shan Shan had been suffering from severe depression over the built-up pressure, and had become suicidal. The evidence was hard to refute, so her father made arrangements for her to withdraw from school. But he refused to give up, even as he signed the paperwork for her withdrawal.

"If she wants to come back, can she enrol again?" he asked.

Looking at his anxiety-ridden face, I couldn't help heaving a silent sigh.

I went to see Shan Shan a few times after she was discharged from the hospital. She was recovering nicely due to the anti-depressants and the relief of not having to study for the exams. Now I could finally feel relieved of my heavy burden.

Nearly six months went by after Shan Shan had withdrawn from school. One day, I was buried in exam papers in the staff room when a dark shadow fell on my desk. I looked up.

"Ah—Shan Shan!" I could not suppress the pleasant surprise in my voice.

Her hair was now cut short with thinly layered ends, which gave her a spirited look. She held the hint of a smile in her jet black eyes.

"Madam Tham, I came back to tell you that I've enrolled in the culinary training programme." Then she put another one of those rustic-looking paper bags on my desk.

"What, eggs again?" I asked with a smile.

"No. It's a byproduct of eggs—a cake. Don't get drunk eating it though, Madam Tham."

"How can you get drunk from eating a cake?"

"I forgot to tell you, I added raisins that have been soaked in strong liquor."

"So this really isn't suitable for children," I said. We both laughed.

"My dad said once I finish the training programme, we'll open a father-and-daughter pastry shop, selling snacks made of eggs."

"Then you can call your shop 'Drunken Eggs'."

"Perfect!" She laughed. "And you'll have to come and host the opening ceremony."

"I'll need a pair of gold scissors."

The brilliant smile on her face made the gentle morning sunlight dance. In her confident smile, I could almost see the bustling future prospects for her Drunken Eggs store.

Ah, the sun had finally come out to replace the rain, and eggs would smile if they had feelings.

Pets

1

A WEEK HAD passed since school started, but Chua Wen Li remained aloof and indifferent in class. One day, I created an entertaining slide show by matching an interesting and lively news item with colourful pictures. It captured the attention of every student. This was the news item: Late one night, an unemployed young man sneaked into a Chinese herbal shop near his home and stole thousands of dollars worth of birds' nests and ginseng to make tonics for his ailing mother. After his arrest, he was tried in court and sentenced to six months in prison. I asked the students to consider the matter from the perspectives of the law, humanity and ethics. Everyone was engaged in an animated discussion and shared their views while Wen Li turned and looked out the window, absent-mindedly playing with the pen in her hand as if she were invisible.

Wen Li had already caught my attention on the second day of the new semester. I had noticed her, not just because she wasn't paying attention in class, but more importantly, because of the mix of expressions on her face: disgust, rebellion and contempt. Obviously she had strong feelings against studying Chinese. I checked her Chinese language exam results in secondary one and two and saw that she had failed the subject in both years. When her name came up, other teachers who had taught her were somewhat hostile. "Wen Li is utterly worthless. She doesn't pay attention in class and her homework is a total mess. When I spoke to her, her attitude couldn't have been worse. She's hopeless, a hard nut to crack," one of the teachers commented.

There is an unknown story inside every tightly shut book, however, and under every glum, dour face is a hidden pain that no one knows about. I decided to have a private chat with her.

She sat before me with a wooden face, emitting a frightening chill, like a block of ice that has remained frozen for thousands of years. Straining to be patient, I asked her in the gentlest voice I could manage, "Wen Li, can you tell me why you dislike studying Chinese?"

She rolled her eyes, revealing nothing but disdain. Anyone else might have been infuriated by such a loathsome expression and insolent reaction, but I had come prepared with steadfast determination to face anything she might say or do. I continued in a gentle voice, "As your form teacher this year, I'd like to get to know you better."

She cast a surprised glance at me, obviously because she had wanted to provoke me but failed to produce the desired result. Nevertheless, she still refused to say a word.

"There are two reasons why someone's Chinese isn't good. One is a weak foundation. The texts are hard to understand and the person falls behind. It becomes a vicious cycle, with the sight of a Chinese text causing an immediate headache," I explained patiently. "The other reason is a lack of interest. When a student treats it only as a subject to be tested on, rote and forced memorisation become the only way to study, which can make the subject even less likeable."

She listened quietly with the same apathetic expression. I paused and threw her a curve ball. "Have you ever had a pet, Wen Li?"

She looked up and despite herself, a hint of gentleness flitted across her face. It took her a while to respond. “Yes,” she said.

“What kind?”

“A turtle.”

“How old is it?”

“It died.” She shrugged.

“From old age?”

“No.”

“Then how did it die?”

“I went to visit my grandma in Malaysia over the holidays,” she said, crinkling her nose. “My mum forgot to feed it and it starved to death.”

“What a shame!”

“It was a shame,” she said. “It was such a lovely turtle.”

“Have you gotten another one?”

“No.”

The stubborn and stiff fifteen-year-old suddenly revealed a rare, tender side when the subject of pets came up. I considered it an extraordinary accomplishment that I’d managed to glimpse a hidden corner of her inner world during our first conversation. In fact, I had my own reason for bringing up the topic of pets with her.

My husband was away in Shanghai for business at the time. Now that I knew the girl liked turtles, I called and asked him to go to the nearby city of Wuxi and bring back one of its unique green-haired turtles, no matter what.

2

Green-haired turtles are one of China’s treasures, which, along with white-jade turtles, two-headed turtles and snake-necked turtles, are known as China's four wondrous turtles. During the Han and Tang Dynasties, raising turtles was popular, and detailed descriptions of green-haired turtles can be found in numerous documents, with references such as "The magnificent turtle grew hair during the Zhou reign" or "A thousand-year-old turtle with hair was a priceless object". During the Tang Dynasty, green-haired turtles were included in the palace's five major treasures. In a nutshell, they were considered precious and rare creatures.

Green-haired turtles, which have a thick layer of hair on their shells, are completely different from common turtles. Their hair is bright green, the colour of emeralds, and soft as velvet. When a green-haired turtle frolics in the water, it looks like a nymph clad in green. A year ago a friend from Wuxi brought me one. A relative's eight-year-old only son fell in love with the turtle and came to see it just about every day. So eventually I reluctantly gave it to him. The relative thanked me profusely, joking that it was all because of that bewitching turtle that her son came home immediately after school every day.

Now the turtle my husband had brought back from Wuxi was swimming leisurely in its tank, its soft hair tinting the clear water a pleasing green. I put it in a small plastic pail with some fresh water and took it to school, where I asked the gardener to keep it for a while.

In our Chinese language class, Wen Li continued to wear her contemptuous look, but I decided not to bother her and just let her be. After class I walked up to her and said softly, "Come with me, Wen Li."

"For what?" she asked, intending to provoke.

She was being unimaginably rude, but I simply replied, "You'll see."

Shoving her chair backwards, Wen Li stood up unhappily and followed me out of the classroom. She dragged her feet and each step was a resounding complaint of anger and annoyance, as she believed some sort of punishment or reprimand awaited her.

I took the pail from the gardener and set it on a stone table in a corner of the school grounds. "Take a look," I said. With suspicion written all over her face, she leaned over and froze after one look.

The green-haired turtle was swimming freely in the pail, displaying its allure and uncommon flair. Morning sunshine streamed through the leaves, dotting the surface of the water with emerald green and silvery lights, while the turtle happily enjoyed the bright morning sun.

The bright lights that shone in Wen Li's eyes were like priceless diamonds. A surprised yet happy smile appeared at the corners of her thin, curved lips. But it could come crashing down at any moment.

"What—what's this?" she asked, finally looking up.

"A turtle," I said with a laugh. "It's a rare species called a green-haired turtle. Isn't it pretty?" She nodded vigorously. "This turtle is for you, Wen Li."

She fixed her gaze on me, eyes filled with disbelief, questioning and irrepressible excitement.

"Be careful though. Green-hair turtles aren't vegetarians, so you have to feed it small fish or shrimps every day. It's a very clever animal and it will recognise you after a while. It'll even respond when you call its name."

"Really?" Now she was smiling not just from her mouth, but from her eyes as well.

"Come, I'll drive you home." I picked up the pail.

She lived in an HDB estate not far from school. When she got out of the car, she walked towards her flat, holding the pail with such care that she might have been carrying the rarest treasure in the world. After a few steps she turned and looked at me. In a nearly inaudible voice, she said, "Thank you."

3

Over the next two weeks, the green-haired turtle became a bridge of communication between us—a shared, intimate topic of conversation.

"Does it eat a lot?" I asked.

"Not too much, but it looks so cute when it eats." She giggled. "I feed it shrimp and it holds them in its hands like a little kid."

"Does it recognise you?"

"I think so, I think it does. It never responds when my mum calls it, but it quickly swims to the surface if I call its name."

"What's its name?"

"Ah—" She smiled, as a glow began to spread across her face. "I'll tell you some other day, all right?"

It was apparent that after we had established this "extracurricular connection", the rebellion and contempt in her eyes was no longer present in class. When I explained the texts, she turned to look out the window less frequently.

One day, I saw her as I was driving through the school gate on my way home after class. I stopped, opened the door, and called out to her, "Jump in, Wen Li. I'll give you a lift."

Naturally, we talked about the turtle.

"Have you found a name for it?" I asked.

She nodded, glanced at me and hesitated before replying, "Smartie."

"Smartie?" I laughed. "Do you want it to take exams some day?"

The smile quickly disappeared from her face.

"I wish it could take my place at the exams."

"Have confidence in yourself, Wen Li."

"But I don't." She lowered her head and her voice grew weaker. "The teachers often call me stupid." Then she looked up and cast a quick glance at me. "I hate my Chinese language teachers most."

I sat there impassively and let her unburden herself.

"I still remember when I was in primary four, every time I failed dictation, my Chinese language teacher would physically punish me by making me pull my ears, squat on the floor and leap like a frog. Everyone in the class treated me like a clown, and when they laughed, I wished I had a knife. Once in primary five, I lost my workbook and the teacher made me stay behind for days after school to make up the exercises. But when I had finally finished all six and turned them in, she tore my workbook into pieces and threw them in my face in front of the whole class. I vowed at that moment I'd never ever study Chinese. My primary six teacher used me as negative example and found an excuse to scold me every day before admonishing everyone against copying my actions, because that would lead to terrible consequences. Since all the Chinese language teachers thought I was hopeless, why shouldn't I prove them right? I didn't listen in class, I didn't read and I didn't study. I couldn't care less if I got a big fat zero on my tests."

The more I heard her speak, the more pain I felt. This was a quintessential vicious cycle. The way the teachers had treated her hurt her deeply, so she went on a study strike in revenge. Worse still, she had stereotyped Chinese language teachers. Convinced that they were all terrible people, she adopted an uncooperative attitude with each of them indiscriminately. Her abominable behaviour, in turn, enraged them to the point that, without exception, they treated her as the class tumour. They never had a kind word or gentle look for her. And the situation worsened each year.

When we reached the car park outside her house, I turned off the engine and said with a smile, "Wen Li, may I go up to visit Smartie?"

"Absolutely!" She was elated by my request.

Both her parents were still at work and the flat was quiet. In the silence, I thought I could hear the green-haired turtle playing in the water. Wen Li had put it in a beautiful glass tank. After taking out a small package of shelled shrimp, she stood by the tank and called out in a tender voice, "Smartie, come. Here, Smartie. Lunch is served." It was a wondrous sight to behold. The smart green-haired turtle quickly floated to the surface when she called out. It looked like a glutton awaiting a gourmet meal. First, the turtle caught the shrimp she had tossed in with its mouth, then it brought its legs together to hold the shrimp so it could take a bite, chew and swallow slowly. It was truly enjoying the meal, as if it was savouring a rare delicacy. Wen Li and I stood on each side of the tank, laughing as we watched the turtle eat. Our laughter seemed to drift into the tank, where it created tiny ripples.

"Madam Tham, do you have a pet?" she asked, still laughing.

"Yes, I do."

"What kind of pet do you have?"

"Words."

"What? Words?" She looked at me with confusion in her eyes.

"Yes, words." I nodded. "Words are my pets. In fact words are like any other pets; they have feelings and emotions. The better you treat them and the closer you get to them, the more ways they find to reward you. When you need vocabulary while speaking or writing, they'll jump up to help you out." I continued with my lesson. "Give it a try,

Wen Li. Put your preconceptions aside and try to study the Chinese language the same way you would raise a pet. Little by little, you'll see that words develop feelings for you when you show your concern."

I took out a book I had purchased beforehand and gave it to her. It was an illustrated copy of *A Hundred Fun Stories with Chinese Idioms*.

"Would you be willing to give this book a chance? There's a lively, interesting story behind every idiom. You can read one story and memorise one idiom a day. Mark the words you don't know with a red pen and I'll help you. Will you do that for me?"

She took the book and flipped through it as the hint of a sweet smile flitted across her face, like a lithe dragonfly skimming over water.

A Fire Rages on the Exam Paper

1

NOT A SINGLE sound could be heard in the large examination hall. This was a life-and-death battle that would determine which students would move on and which would be held back. So understandably everyone was focused, heads buried in their exam papers, hands writing frantically. It was so quiet that all one heard were the rustling noises made by pens scratching paper. Upon closer examination, the scratching seemed to resemble the sound of clashing weapons, shrouding the room with the serious and solemn air of combat.

As form teacher of Secondary 1A, I served as one of the exam invigilators. Walking around the room, I was constantly on the move, but I never took my eyes off Kwa Yao Zu. Sitting up straight, he wore a deep frown as his eyes swept anxiously up and down the exam booklet. The room was air-conditioned, but that didn't stop beads of perspiration from forming on his forehead as a dark, glum patina shrouded his fair, genteel face. I picked a discreet corner to stand in, and watched quietly as he was assailed by anxiety and apprehension. But I was helpless to give him any assistance.

Ai, the boy was probably having another bout of exam-phobia.

To be honest, my first impression of Yao Zu had been extremely positive. Tall and slender, with long legs that were held straight and close together, he was not a talkative student. His serene eyes always demonstrated undivided attention when he was listening to me in class. When I wasn't speaking, however, his eyes would betray his preoccupation with other thoughts. Due to his mature and calm demeanour, he stood out amongst the group of hyperactive, boisterous students. Hence he was the logical choice for class monitor when the students elected their class committee members.

Methodical in everything he did, he performed all his tasks well, and often volunteered for work that wasn't required of him. What I appreciated most was his serious and diligent approach to his studies. His homework, for instance, was flawless and he presented detailed and convincing arguments to analytical questions, fully demonstrating the clarity of his thinking.

It seemed logical that such a student would come out on top in tests and exams. Reality, however, showed that I couldn't have been more mistaken.

In April the school held an important common test. He did terribly, failing every one of the three required and three elective subjects.

Surprised rather than upset, I asked him to see me in the staff room. He hung his head without speaking. When I asked him what was wrong, he refused to talk about it and apologised profusely.

"I'm so sorry, Madam Tham. I'll do better next time."

I called his home and asked his mother to come and see me. She was in her forties, but looked much older. Her age did not manifest itself superficially in the form of wrinkles, but in her worn-out expression. It was a sad sight to behold. With a pair of lifeless eyes, her face was like a pit after the meaty fruit around it had been sucked dry. Yet she startled me when she opened her mouth, for she rambled on and on incoherently.

"With Yao Zu in this state, you have no idea how much pain it would bring his father. I'm utterly worthless and it makes no difference whether I'm alive or dead. Sometimes I wish I could switch places with his father. I tell Yao Zu all the time to study hard. If he doesn't, he'll disappoint his father. But now, what's the use of studying hard? His father's gone. I'm so useless I can't even take care of a child."

Yao Zu was quiet the whole time, watching his mother with a tender, concerned gaze.

"When did your father pass away, Yao Zu?" I turned to ask him.

"Last year."

"Due to an illness?"

He shook his head. "An airplane crash. He was on a business trip to Indonesia."

I did recall hearing about a plane flying to Singapore from Indonesia that had crashed into a river. Who would have thought that his father would be one of the victims? Maybe his mother had aged so drastically because she had yet to recover from the heartrending grief. Perhaps Yao Zu had been so deeply affected that he was having trouble concentrating during his exams. What I could not understand was, why would such an outstanding student perform so poorly only during tests and exams? His recent test scores were so appalling, they couldn't simply be attributed to emotional distress or anxiety.

I tried talking to him several times after that day, but he clammed up like a walnut. He was impossible to pry open, except for a repeated promise: "I'll work hard, Madam Tham, I will."

No matter how hard he worked, however, he still came up short during tests and exams.

Illness in the heart can only be treated from the inside. There had to be a dark shadow deep inside him, but how could I root out the demon that had taken hold of his heart if he refused to open up?

2

Not long after that, an opportunity presented itself. A renowned magazine was sponsoring an essay contest for all the students in the country. It had a creative topic: "The Shadow of a Snake in a Cup: On My Fears."

This was a reference to a classical Chinese literary allusion. A person who is afraid of snakes is likely to mistake the shadow of an archery bow in a cup for a snake.

I did my best to urge my students to participate.

"Writing is sometimes more effective than therapy," I suggested meaningfully. "If you can write frankly about your fears, that means you are able to confront your problems head-on. A person who can face problems calmly can often lance festering internal sores, and find solutions to problems that have been lurking for a long time." Then I ended on a lighter note. "The contest comes with a hefty cash prize. See what an incredible bargain it is—by speaking honestly about your fears, you can receive a monetary reward."

Everyone but Yao Zu laughed. He remained expressionless.

More than a week passed, and by then quite a few students had turned in their essays. But Yao Zu had not made a move, so I switched tactics and forced him into doing so.

"Everyone, I've decided that you all have to submit an essay for the competition," I announced in class. "In ten days, not a day later."

Yao Zu waited until the last day to hand in his essay. His expression was solemn.

"I have a request, Madam Tham."

I nodded for him to go on.

"This essay is for your eyes only," he said, dead serious. "I don't want to submit it to the contest."

I agreed to his request. As soon as I reached the staff room, I began to read his essay. It was long and the writing was sloppy, a clear sign of his inner turmoil. Tears welled up in my eyes as I read on. What a tormented child.

One long section of the essay went like this:

"The plane crash not only snatched away my father's life but on a certain level, took my mother's along with it. And mine, of course. My mother is no longer the woman who once wore a smile all the time. She's become moody and agitated. One minute she'll nag me to study hard to comfort my father's spirit in heaven and the next she'll be dismissive of hard work, since it can't bring my father back. Everything in life is pointless, including life itself, which is transient and an illusion. She'll be saying all this to me and begin to cry bitterly. There is never a peaceful moment at home. My emotional response to a mother like this is complex. Sometimes I want to cover my ears and escape from her; sometimes I feel like running away from home; sometimes I want to just grab her by the shoulders and shake her until she wakes up and walks out of her dark world to live again; but most of the time, I watch quietly and let her vent. The person we both loved so deeply is gone, and now I'm all she has, so I must be a strong support for her. I can't hurt her. I can't, I simply can't. My mother is different now and so am I. I'm no longer the same confident person I once was. In the past, I always believed I would have everything under my control so long as I was well prepared. But look at my father, he was a man who knew what to do and had everything planned out, and yet, he had no control over his own life. The day before he left for his trip, he smiled and said to me, "We'll all go to Taiwan over the December school holidays." But in an instant, that lively person vanished like flying dust and dying ashes, leaving no trace behind. We had a major exam a month after my father died. When I opened the exam booklet, for some unknown reason, I saw balls of raging fire roiling and rolling all over the page. My mind was a blank and all I wanted to do was run away, run to some far-off place. I struggled to finish the exam, but I was exhausted from terror. I'd always gotten the best exam results in the past, but this time I barely passed. Now, even after entering secondary school, the terror continues to pursue me like a demon. I'm afraid. I'm really afraid that my life is over."

Clutching Yao Zu's essay, I felt like I was seeing a helpless soul sobbing in pain. He didn't know that he was suffering from psychological trauma, and was struggling vainly and all alone in a dark abyss. Sadly his mother was in worse shape than he was, and she had no intention of seeking professional help.

I had a long talk with him the next day and stressed the importance of therapy for both mother and son. With help from the school, I arranged for him to meet with a therapist once a week and suggested that he send his mother to a hospital for formal therapy.

A few weeks later, I checked on him. He said with a smile that his mother had been taking anti-depressants and had accepted her therapist's suggestion to volunteer at a nursing home. Now that she had expanded her circle of daily life, there were fewer chances for her to be preoccupied with all sorts of wild thoughts, and as a result, she was no longer as incoherent as before.

Now that his mother was getting better, I assumed that the son would also make real progress. When I asked the resident therapist,

I was surprised to learn that she was having trouble entering Yao Zu's inner world, since he was so reluctant to talk. On those rare occasions when he did speak, he was flawlessly polite and brimming with confidence, the opposite of someone in need of psychological help.

I was not fooled, however; Yao Zu had problems. I was sure of that. His problems would show up as soon as he entered an exam room. But what could I do to help rid him of the demon in his heart?

3

I happened upon a documentary film one day.

It was about training elephants in a circus. The trainer tied a baby elephant to a big, thick post. The elephant struggled with all its might, but could not move an inch. Then the trainer tied it to a smaller post, and still the elephant could not break free. A few days later, the trainer used a much smaller post, and again the elephant tried, to no avail. As time went on, the elephant came to the conclusion that it could never break free from the wooden post or anything resembling one. Once such reasoning had formed in its head, it would never try to break free again because of its previous repeated failures—even though by now it had grown into an elephant strong enough to break free. In other words, it gave up on itself. By this time, even a small post was sufficient to subdue an adult elephant. Thus, without much trouble, the trainer could control an animal that weighed several tonnes and make it perform all sorts of difficult tasks without meeting any resistance.

My mind raced after I watched the documentary. The elephant feared a post simply because of a dark shadow in its mind. Although the shadow itself possessed no real power, it was potent enough to wear away the animal's courage, to the point where humans could enslave it for the rest of its life. What terrified and worried Yao Zu most was a similarly shadowy illusion. He was being helplessly eaten away by habitual fear. It almost seemed as though the film had been shot specifically for him.

After countless phone calls, I finally got hold of a copy of the film from a friend. The exams were only a week away, so I handed it to Yao Zu the next day.

"Watch this carefully, Yao Zu," I said prudently. "Watch it more than once. You'll find it very helpful."

He returned the film a few days later, looking like it had made an impact on him. I was comforted by the happy impression that thought-provoking pictures and stories sometimes work better on an intelligent person than straightforward didacticism.

When I saw cold sweat pouring down his pale face in the examination hall, however, I felt my heart plummet. After much hesitation, I made up my mind and walked up to the chief invigilator.

"The student over there," I said in a low voice, pointing to Yao Zu, "is having an anxiety attack. I'd like to take him outside for some fresh air."

One look told the invigilator that something was wrong. He nodded, giving his permission. I strode over and gently rapped on the boy's desk. He looked up at me.

"Come with me, Yao Zu," I whispered.

Putting down his pen, he followed me outside, where we were surrounded by the sight of cool and pleasing greenery. Slender bamboo stood in a corner of the campus.

We walked over and I pointed at an unusually long, thin bamboo pole.

"Use your imagination, Yao Zu. Imagine that you are a powerful elephant. A tiny bamboo pole like this is no match for you. Go on, break free from it. You can do it. I know you can."

He stood there quietly for a while before finally saying, "I'd like to return to the exam hall, Madam Tham."

We went back inside and I walked off as soon as he sat down. When I turned to look a moment later, he was wiping his sweaty forehead with a handkerchief.

Acknowledgments

I would like to thank Taiwan's *Living Psychology* magazine for publishing the original collection of short stories reflecting the issues facing Singapore's youth.

My gratitude also goes to Edmund Wee, the founder of Epigram Books, for publishing *Teaching Cats to Jump Hoops* and for allowing these short stories to take on a different voice in a different language, to Dr. Chua Chee Lay for his valuable insights and opinions, and finally to my daughter, Jacinta Lim Ke Jun, for her time and effort spent on reading and suggesting improvements to the manuscript.